The Best of
60s TV

MALLARD
PRESS

An imprint of BDD Promotional Book Company, Inc.,
666 Fifth Avenue, New York, New York 10103

Photographs from the Photofest collection

The Best of 60s TV

Michael McCall

Previous pages: (l. to r.) the cast of Sesame Street; Robert Vaughn in The Man from U.N.C.L.E.; Barbara Parkins and Ryan O'Neal of Peyton Place; the cast of Star Trek. These pages: (left) Raymond Burr in Ironside; (right) Joe Flynn in McHale's Navy.

MALLARD PRESS

AN IMPRINT OF BDD PROMOTIONAL BOOK COMPANY, INC.
666 FIFTH AVENUE
NEW YORK, N.Y. 10103

MALLARD PRESS AND THE ACCOMPANYING DUCK LOGO ARE REGISTERED TRADEMARKS OF THE BDD PROMOTIONAL BOOK COMPANY, INC. REGISTERED IN THE U.S. PATENT OFFICE, COPYRIGHT © 1992.

FIRST PUBLISHED IN THE UNITED STATES OF AMERICA IN 1992 BY THE MALLARD PRESS.

ALL RIGHTS RESERVED.

Copyright © 1992 by M & M Books

ISBN 0-7924-5831-1

AN M&M BOOK
The Best of 60s TV was prepared and produced by M & M Books, 11 W. 19th Street, New York, New York 10011.

Project Director & Editor Gary Fishgall
Editorial Assistants Maxine Dormer, Ben D'Amprisi, Jr.
Copyediting and Proofreading Judith Rudnicki
Designer David Lunn
Separations and Printing Regent Publishing Services Ltd.

All of the photos in this volume are courtesy of Photofest, except for that on page 62, which is courtesy of Vernon J. Biever Photo, and that on page 65, which is courtesy of NASA.

-CONTENTS-

4. Situation Comedies / 69

5. Variety Shows / 99

Acknowledgements / 112

Tom Smothers (left) and Dick Smothers of The Smothers Brothers Comedy Hour.

Introduction

At the start of the 1960s, network television was a precocious teen-ager. Television sets had existed since the 1930s, but the idea of broadcasting daily programs across the country only took off after RCA began mass producing a seven-inch TV screen in 1947. That year, the RCA-owned NBC network began broadcasting programs which, like the radio shows before them, aired each week on specific days at specific times.

By 1960, television sets were as common to the American home as refrigerators and stoves. The novelty may have worn off, but TV's role as a central entertainment medium was growing. It wasn't only a contraption that families gathered around and watched intently, as if attending a movie. It was becoming a device that people turned on as they completed household chores, ate dinner, and fell asleep. By the end of the 1960s, the average American watched more than six hours of TV a day. It had become an indelible part of the fabric of American life.

The decade started with television playing a major role in electing a president, John F. Kennedy. Three years later, it ran footage of the same president's assassination, then canceled all commercial programming and advertisements in order to keep a shocked nation informed of developments. Two days after the assassination, millions of people viewed a murder as it happened when JFK's alleged assassin, Lee Harvey Oswald, was gunned down while being transferred to a federal prison.

TV carried men, women, and children to war in Vietnam and took the whole world to the moon alongside the Apollo XI astronauts. It captured political riots at the Democratic convention in Chicago and race riots exploding in several cities across the country.

TV supplied diversion from the real world, too. As the decade started, cowboys still ruled the airwaves. In 1960, 26 Western series were part of the weekly fare. But the horse operas faded fast. By 1963, only eight remained in production.

The rugged was replaced by the ridiculous. As situation comedies began to dominate prime time, the networks relied increasingly on shows centered around gimmicks and/or broad comic characters. There were the hayseeds transplanted into novel settings in *The Beverly Hillbillies*, *Gomer Pyle,* and *Gilligan's Island*; there were the otherworldly beings settled into Middle American communities in *My Favorite Martian*, *Bewitched*, *I Dream of Jeannie*, *The Addams Family*, and *The Munsters*; there were comic superheroes (*Batman*), comic stone-age families (*The Flintstones*), and comic talking animals (*Mister Ed*); there were even comedies set in wartime (*McHale's Navy*, *Hogan's Heroes*).

Amid all the absurd premises and bizarre characters, an occasional situation comedy emerged with people who seemed somewhat real, or at least like folks the average viewer might want to get to know. *The Andy Griffith Show* and *The Dick Van Dyke Show*, one based in a rural community and the other in an urban area, introduced memorable characters to the American public. They also set new standards for warmly humorous writing in 30-minute serial programs.

Of course, not every 1960 series was funny. Medical programs, like *Dr. Kildare*, *Ben Casey*, and *Marcus Welby, M. D.*, focused on dedicated healers dealing with the medical and emotional traumas of their patients. Crime shows were increasingly popular. Some, like *Mission Impossible*, featured intricate schemes for foiling the world's dictators and despots. Others, like *The F.B.I.*, *Hawaii Five-O*, *Mannix*, and *Ironside* dealt with dedicated crimebusters—on the force or in private practice—in pursuit of more mundane lawbreakers. Still, some government agents found time for laughs. The guys from *I Spy* didn't take themselves too seriously, *The Avengers* and *The Man from U.N.C.L.E.* were decidedly hip, and Maxwell Smart gave new meaning to "chaos."

Jethro (Max Baer, Jr., left) and Jed (Buddy Ebsen) of The Beverly Hillbillies, with a small portion of their $25 million.

The 1960s were turbulent years in America and by the latter part of the decade, television had begun to respond to the social changes taking place in the culture. The racial barrier started to crumble when Bill Cosby co-starred in *I Spy* and Diahann Carroll appeared as the lead character in *Julia*. Similarly, *That Girl* joined *Julia* in depicting independent, single women pursuing careers and providing for themselves. *Mod Squad* made three hippie-like characters its leads. And *The Smothers Brothers Comedy Hour* and *Rowan & Martin's Laugh-In* reflected the humor of the 1960s counter-culture.

Today, the images of the 1960s remain with us. Thanks to syndication and cable channels, we can still watch Rob Petrie trip over the ottoman and Gomer Pyle progress from a Mayberry gas station attendant to a wide-eyed Marine recruit. Samantha Stevens still twitches her nose to cast bewitching spells, and Mister Ed still talks horse sense to his reluctant owner. Steed and Emma Peel continue to solve capers fashionably, and Fred Flintstone still roars "Yabba-Dabba-Do!"

In the 1960s, television rose to new heights of significance and silliness. It became a regular member of the American family.

Dramatic Series

Defendant Sam Jaffe (center) doesn't look too worried about his case. Perhaps that's because he knows that his litigators are Preston & Preston, the formidable father-son team played by E. G. Marshall (left) and Robert Reed.

(Preceding page) William Shatner as Capt. James T. Kirk (left) and Leonard Nimoy as Mr. Spock in *Star Trek*.

The Defenders

The Defenders, the story of father-and-son law partners, grew out of a critically acclaimed, two-part story presented in 1957 by the anthology series, *Studio One*. Four years later, CBS turned the idea into a prime-time series.

Tough, seasoned Lawrence Preston (E. G. Marshall) and his headstrong son, Ivy League law school graduate Kenneth Preston (Robert Reed), had just formed the firm of Preston & Preston as the series began. The two were courtroom advocates willing to take on difficult cases, which enabled them to confront such controversial legal issues as mercy killing, abortion, political blacklisting, and the rights of immigrants. On occasion, the team even lost a case.

The first season featured two other regular cast members: the firm's secretary, Helen Donaldson (Polly Rowles), and Kenneth's girlfriend, Joan Hackett. By the second season, however, the women were gone, and the plots spent more time dealing sensitively with the relationship and generational differences between father and son. As the series evolved, the younger Preston matured, his father's lessons teaching him the difference between legal theory and reality. The program won 13 Emmy awards during its four seasons, including two consecutive honors for Marshall for Outstanding Continued Performance by an Actor in a Series.

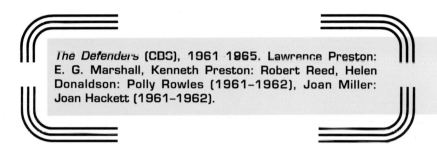

The Defenders (CBS), 1961–1965. Lawrence Preston: E. G. Marshall, Kenneth Preston: Robert Reed, Helen Donaldson: Polly Rowles (1961–1962), Joan Miller: Joan Hackett (1961–1962).

Here, Lawrence Preston (Marshall) makes an impassioned plea to the jury. The actor won back-to-back Emmys for his work as the dedicated attorney.

Ben Casey

For the moment all eyes seem to be on the talented but strong-willed neurosurgeon of County General Hospital, Ben Casey (Vince Edwards, right). Casey's co-workers are (l. to r.) Bettye Ackerman as Dr. Maggie Graham, Sam Jaffe as Dr. David Zorba, and Harry Landers as Dr. Ted Hoffman.

Here, Casey (Edwards, left) pays a post-op visit to a patient played by veteran film actor Melvin Douglas. The episode, "Rage Against the Dying Light," originally aired in March 1963.

In an era dominated by sitcoms and police shows, *Ben Casey*, along with *Dr. Kildare*, launched a popular new television genre, the medical drama. Both shows debuted in 1961 and quickly established strong followings, thanks largely to adult women, who tuned in to follow the exploits of the intense, handsome leading characters. Both series lasted five years, with drastic changes in their last seasons leading to their demise.

Ben Casey was played by Vince Edwards, an actor discovered by series producer Bing Crosby. A brain surgeon at County General Hospital, Casey seemed endowed with prodigious knowledge sweeping across all medical disciplines, but when faced with a crisis, he often turned for moral guidance to his fatherly mentor, Dr. David Zorba (Sam Jaffe). He also enjoyed the understanding support of veteran anesthesiologist Dr. Maggie Graham (Bettye Ackerman).

The weekly introduction set the sober, serious tone for the series, as an announcer ominously stated: "Man, woman, birth, death, infinity," while the screen displayed the symbol for each word. The episode that followed usually unfolded with white-knuckled tension and occasionally focused on a socially controversial subject.

In 1965, the program underwent major surgery, introducing several new characters. Dr. Zorba left, to be replaced by a new chief surgeon, Dr. Daniel Freeland (Franchot Tone). And Casey developed his first romantic relationship, with Jane Hancock (Stella Stevens), who had awakened after 13 years in a coma. The series was canceled at the end of the season.

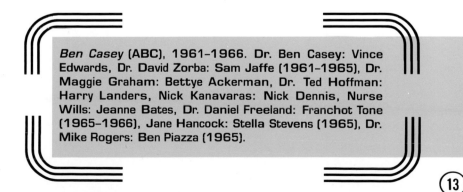

Ben Casey (ABC), 1961-1966. Dr. Ben Casey: Vince Edwards, Dr. David Zorba: Sam Jaffe (1961-1965), Dr. Maggie Graham: Bettye Ackerman, Dr. Ted Hoffman: Harry Landers, Nick Kanavaras: Nick Dennis, Nurse Wills: Jeanne Bates, Dr. Daniel Freeland: Franchot Tone (1965-1966), Jane Hancock: Stella Stevens (1965), Dr. Mike Rogers: Ben Piazza (1965).

With their hair barely mussed and their ties still impeccably knotted, those wily, sophisticated men from U.N.C.L.E. are in hot pursuit of their archenemies from THRUSH. Russian-born Illya Kuryakin (David McCallum) leads the way with Napoleon Solo (Robert Vaughn) right behind.

The Man from U.N.C.L.E.

Napoleon Solo, the central character of the NBC series, *The Man from U.N.C.L.E.*, first appeared as a sinister character in the James Bond story, *Goldfinger*. When television producer Norman Felton decided to create a lighthearted program that imitated the outlandish doings of 007, he contacted Bond creator Ian Fleming and received permission to use Solo's name.

Solo, played by Robert Vaughn, was transformed into an intrepid super agent assigned to a secret government agency, U.N.C.L.E. (United Network Command for Law and Enforcement). Like Bond, Solo was sophisticated, dashing, and droll. His Russian-born sidekick, Illya Kuryakin (David McCallum), was introspective and athletic. Together, they spent most of their time outfoxing a diabolically evil syndicate, THRUSH, which was bent on taking over the world. A recurring element in a number of episodes was the heroic agents' reliance upon average citizens for help during their adventures. Solo and Kuryakin traveled the world, but the secret, futuristic U.N.C.L.E. headquarters were in New York. Heading the office was Alexander Waverly (Leo G. Carroll), who gave the duo their assignments and helped coordinate their endeavors. The program debuted in 1964, but by its third year, the plot twists had grown absurdly silly. That same season, a spinoff program, *The Girl from U.N.C.L.E.*, was introduced and seemed to burn out the audience. *Girl* only lasted a year. *The Man from U.N.C.L.E.* ended in 1968.

The Man from U.N.C.L.E. (NBC), 1964–1968. Napoleon Solo: Robert Vaughn, Illya Kuryakin: David McCallum, Alexander Waverly: Leo G. Carroll, Lisa Rogers: Barbara Moore (1967–1968).

Back at U.N.C.L.E. headquarters in New York, Kuryakin and Solo (McCallum, left, and Vaughn, right) get directions from their boss, Alexander Waverly, played by Leo G. Carroll of <u>Topper</u> fame.

Mr. Novak successfully took the television drama into the American classroom. James Franciscus, who had previously starred as a young policeman in *Naked City*, portrayed a dedicated, somewhat unconventional high school English instructor, John Novak. The series followed him on his first job at Jefferson High School, where the idealistic teacher confronted the challenges, combatted the disappointments, and quietly cherished the achievements of a public school educator. He battled both the apathy of his students and the narrow-minded doctrines of his superiors.

Mr. Novak also featured two acclaimed character actors, Dean Jagger and Burgess Meredith. Jagger portrayed Jefferson High principal Albert Vane, a firm, wise man who originally clashed with Novak but eventually became his supporter and mentor, although he still occasionally disputed the younger teacher's methods.

At the start of the second year, Vane was promoted to state superintendent of schools. As his high school replacement, he appointed English teacher Martin Woodridge (Meredith), a new character. Both Novak and Woodridge regularly turned to the superintendent for advice and for help in disputes.

The trio headed a large cast of teachers and students, most of whom surfaced only periodically. The cast was altered significantly between the first season and the second, final year.

Mr. Novak

Mr. Novak (NBC), 1963–1965. John Novak: James Franciscus, Albert Vane: Dean Jagger, Martin Woodridge: Burgess Meredith (1964–1965), Jean Pagano: Jeanne Bal (1963–1964), Jerry Allen: Steve Franken (1963–1964), Marilyn Scott: Marian Collier, Everett Johns: André Phillippe, Pete Butler: Vince Howard, Stan Peeples: Stephen Roberts, Ann Floyd: Kathleen Ellis, Rosemary Dorsey: Marjorie Corley (1964–1965), Ruth Wilkinson: Phyllis Avery (1964–1965), Arthur Bradwell: William Zuckert (1964–1965), Paul Webb: David Sheiner (1964–1965).

Mission: Impossible

Each episode of *Mission: Impossible* began the same way, with one of the most stylized, memorable, and most frequently parodied introductions in TV history. The head of an exceptional team of undercover U.S. agents, known collectively as the Impossible Missions Force (IMF), would obtain a cassette tape with a recorded message detailing an assignment for him to think over. Each message would end with: "Your mission, should you decide to accept it, is . . . this tape will self-destruct in five seconds." Then the cassette would melt in a cloud of smoke. Thereafter, the leader would select the team of agents for that particular assignment by paging through the photos of the full IMF roster. Of course he always picked the same ones—the show's regulars—plus an occasional guest star.

The missions usually involved Communist groups bent on disrupting the world or overtaking America, and the IMF's schemes for foiling these plots were outlandishly intricate, usually involving the use of disguises and high-tech gadgetry, and requiring split-second execution. When the hour-long series debuted on CBS in 1967, Steven Hill was the chief agent, Daniel Briggs. He was replaced the following year by Peter Graves, as Jim Phelps.

Phelps' partners included smooth electronics expert Barney Collier (Greg Morris); master of disguises Rollin Hand (Martin Landau); seductive, versatile Cinnamon Carter (Barbara Bain); and quiet muscle-man Willy Armitage (Peter Lupus). Landau and Bain, husband and wife at the time, left the show in 1969 over a contract dispute. Their replacements, all short term, included Leonard Nimoy, Lesley Ann Warren, Sam Elliott, and Lynda Day George. The show ran for seven years, ending in 1973.

Their missions—if they chose to accept them—were to seek out and destroy dictators and despots the world over. They were the Impossible Missions Force: (l. to r.) Peter Lupus, Barbara Bain, Greg Morris, Martin Landau, and Peter Graves.

The Virginian

The Virginian (NBC), 1962–1971. (original cast) The Virginian: James Drury, Trampas: Doug McClure, Judge Henry Garth: Lee J. Cobb (1962–1966), Betsy Garth: Roberta Shore (1962–1965), Molly Wood: Pippa Scott (1962–1963), Steve: Gary Clarke (1962–1964).

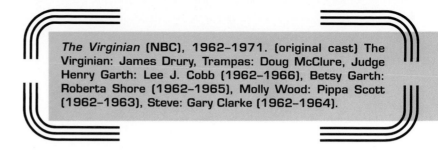

The *Virginian* originally galloped into American popular culture in Owen Wister's classic novel of the same name, published in 1902. Thereafter, several movies based on the character were produced, including a well-known 1929 version starring Gary Cooper and Walter Huston.

Actor James Drury first took *The Virginian* role in a television pilot in the 1950s. He was cast as a foppish dandy with lace cuffs and skin-tight pants tucked into gleaming leather boots. The show failed, but in 1962 Drury re-emerged in the NBC series as the reliable but somewhat taciturn ranch foreman known only as the Virginian.

The Virginian, the first 90-minute Western series, was set at the expansive Shiloh Ranch in Medicine Bow, Wyoming, where the lead character sought refuge while struggling with advancing civilization from the east and the changes it imposed on western life.

Besides Drury, the other primary cast member was Doug McClure as a young, coltish cowhand called Trampas, the name of the Virginian's principal foe in the novel. The ranch where the two worked endured a succession of owners: Judge Henry Garth (Lee J. Cobb), brothers John and Clay Grainger (Charles Bickford and John McIntire), and finally Col. Alan MacKenzie (Stewart Granger).

After eight years, including several in which the series ranked among TV's Top 20 programs, the series was re-titled *The Men from Shiloh* and the historical period was moved forward to the beginning of the 20th century.

James Drury was the show's title character, the reliable but somewhat taciturn ranch foreman with no name. He and Doug McClure were the only actors to stay with the show throughout its nine-year run.

The first owner of Shiloh Ranch was Judge Henry Garth (Lee J. Cobb), a widower with a fiery teenage daughter, Betsy (Roberta Shore). Here they are engaged in conversation with Betsy's teacher, played by Pippa Scott.

Although they were extremely effective, the dapper Jonathan Steed (Patrick Macnee) and the sleek, sexy Emma Peel (Diana Rigg) made an unlikely pair of secret agents.

The Avengers

The Avengers (ABC), 1966–1969. Jonathan Steed: Patrick Macnee, Emma Peel: Diana Rigg (1966–1968), Tara King: Linda Thorson (1968–1969), "Mother": Patrick Newell (1968–1969).

The Avengers began in 1961 as a British television series about a man seeking his wife's murderers. Assigned to join him in his investigation was Jonathan Steed, a sophisticated, smartly dressed secret agent played with whimsical perfection by Patrick Macnee. Steed proved an audience favorite, and by the second year he took over as the program's lead character. That season he was joined by a female partner, originally played by Honor Blackman, the actress who had starred as Pussy Galore in the James Bond movie, *Goldfinger.*

In 1966, the popular series crossed the Atlantic Ocean to join the ABC prime-time lineup. By then, Steed had acquired a new partner, Emma Peel (Diana Rigg), whose sleek sensuality and preference for 1960s mod leather and boots proved a fine foil for the senior agent. Among TV's first liberated women, Peel delivered a wicked karate chop and had brains as well as beauty.

Week after week, the partners cleverly thwarted diabolical villains in the series' fanciful plots. The relationship between Steed and Peel remained allusive, limited to quick-witted quips and coy flirting. It had been established in an early episode that she was the widow of a test pilot. In March 1968, her husband reappeared and Peel left the agency to join him, replaced by 20-year-old Tara King (Linda Thorson). That season, Steed also gained a superior, a wheelchair-bound man known as "Mother." The show was canceled in 1969.

After two years, Diana Rigg left The Avengers and Steed got a new partner, Linda Thorson, who played Tara King. But the show was canceled at the end of the season.

At the end of the first season, Constance MacKenzie (Dorothy Malone) finally married Elliott Carson (Tim O'Connor), the real father of her illegitimate daughter, Allison, after Carson was released from prison.

Peyton Place

The first successful prime-time soap opera, *Peyton Place*, was based on the best-selling novel of the same name by Grace Metalious. It had also inspired a popular 1957 movie and several sequels. ABC opened the series in 1964 with two different 30-minute telecasts a week, and both segments ranked among the year's Top 20 programs. The network expanded the airings to three times a week in 1965, then returned to the twice weekly format the following season.

Peyton Place was a small New England town repeatedly ripped apart by tragedies and rife with sordid affairs and dark secrets. Initially, the show revolved around three families: bookshop owner Constance MacKenzie (Dorothy Malone) and her secretly illegitimate daughter, Allison MacKenzie (Mia Farrow); wealthy Leslie Harrington (Paul Langton) and his sons, Rodney (Ryan O'Neal) and Norman (Chris Connelly); and George and Julie Anderson (Henry Beckman, Kasey Rogers) and their daughter, Betty (Barbara Parkins). Other major characters were Dr. Michael Rossi (Ed Nelson) and attorney Steven Cord (James Douglas).

The show launched the careers of Farrow, who stayed for only two seasons, and O'Neal, who remained until the end in 1969. In all, the ABC cast list included more than a hundred regulars over the years. Others featured in short-lived roles included Mariette Hartley, Leslie Nielsen, Lee Grant, David Canary, Leigh Taylor-Young, Gena Rowlands, Dan Duryea, Barbara Rush, Ruby Dee, Glynn Turman, and Joyce Jillson.

Peyton Place (ABC), (1964–1969). (original cast) Constance MacKenzie: Dorothy Malone, Allison MacKenzie: Mia Farrow (1964–1966), Leslie Harrington: Paul Langton (1964–1968), Rodney Harrington: Ryan O'Neal, Norman Harrington: Chris Connelly, Betty Anderson: Barbara Parkins, Julie Anderson: Kasey Rogers, George Anderson: Henry Beckman (1964–1965), Dr. Michael Rossi: Ed Nelson, Steven Cord: James Douglas, Eli Carson: Frank Ferguson.

Peyton Place introduced America to (l. to r.) Mia Farrow, as Allison MacKenzie; Barbara Parkins, who played Betty Anderson; and Ryan O'Neal, as Rodney Harringon, but Farrow stayed with the series for only two years.

Drawn from the files of the bureau itself, *The F.B.I.* focused on the cases of a fictional inspector, Lewis Erskine, played by Efrem Zimbalist, Jr. He is seen here, at left, with William Reynolds (right) as Agent Tom Colby and guest star Tim O'Connor as an airline hijacker.

The F.B.I.

The U.S. Federal Bureau of Investigation has served as the inspiration for several radio and television series, but only *The F.B.I.* gained the endorsement of long-time bureau director J. Edgar Hoover. The Quinn Martin production, which began in 1965, claimed to base its weekly dramas on real agency cases, in all instances depicting its investigators as incorruptible professionals. For some scenes, Hoover even granted access to F.B.I. headquarters in Washington, D.C. In turn, the producers concluded each episode with a no-nonsense description and mug shot of a fugitive from the agency's most-wanted list.

Efrem Zimbalist, Jr. played the lead role of Inspector Lewis Erskine. With dispassionate authority,

Erskine methodically gathered evidence each week that enabled him to capture spies, extortionists, anti-government radicals, counterfeiters, mobsters, and other perpetrators of federal crimes. Erskine reported to Arthur Ward (Philip Abbott), the assistant F.B.I. director with whom the inspector rarely clashed. During the first season, viewers saw something of Erskine's home life. He had a daughter, Barbara (Lynn Loring), but she was written out thereafter, and the agent never again referred to his family or his friends during the remaining eight seasons of the show's run. Of Erskine's several partners over the years, William Reynolds as Agent Tom Colby served the longest stint. Other than Ward and Erskine, the other prominent roles belonged to the agency's gleaming Ford sedans, supplied by the program's primary sponsor.

The series lasted until 1974 and stands as ABC's longest-running crime drama.

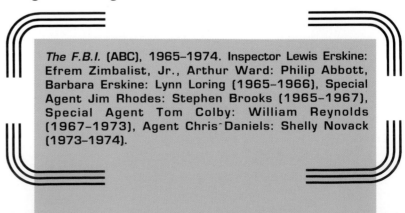

The F.B.I. (ABC), 1965–1974. Inspector Lewis Erskine: Efrem Zimbalist, Jr., Arthur Ward: Philip Abbott, Barbara Erskine: Lynn Loring (1965–1966), Special Agent Jim Rhodes: Stephen Brooks (1965–1967), Special Agent Tom Colby: William Reynolds (1967–1973), Agent Chris Daniels: Shelly Novack (1973–1974).

The Prisoner

The Prisoner is widely considered one of the most original and creative series to appear on prime-time television. Although the hour-long fantasy drama lasted only two summer seasons on CBS, it maintains a large cult following thanks to a syndicated PBS revival and videocassette recordings.

Created by lead actor Patrick McGoohan, who also wrote and directed many episodes, the series told the story of a former English government agent who was kidnapped after resigning his position. He was held in a scenic community located on a lush peninsula with rolling green hills and well-kept parks and gardens (the setting was actually a resort in North Wales). Whenever the prisoner neared the perimeter, he was pushed back by one of the sinister white spheres that floated overhead.

McGoohan, known only as Number 6, defied the brainwashing that turned many of the locals—former government officials like himself—into peacefully vacant captives, content with life in the spooky village. He could not trust these vacuous residents, as some of them were spies working for the mysterious leader, Number 1, who resided in a beautiful castle in the middle of the peninsula. Number 6's lone confidant was a mute servant known only as Butler.

In the final episode, Number 6 was invited into the castle, which turned out to be a trap, yet another attempt to subdue him. This time, however, he, Butler, and two other rebels were able to escape. In their wake, the castle was demolished and their captors killed.

After resigning his position in government, the Prisoner (Patrick McGoohan) was kidnapped and taken to a quaint but bizarre village where all the men dressed as he is attired here.

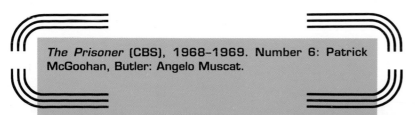

The Prisoner (CBS), 1968–1969. Number 6: Patrick McGoohan, Butler: Angelo Muscat.

Jack Lord was Steve McGarrett, the leader of a special police unit known as Five-O. Even in threatening situations, such as the one pictured here, viewers couldn't help but revel in the lush locale where the series was shot.

For 11 of <u>Hawaii Five-O</u>'s 12 seasons, James MacArthur, the son of celebrated actress Helen Hayes, portrayed McGarrett's top assistant, Danny "Dano" Williams. The guest actress on the left is Antoinette Bower.

Hawaii Five-O

The name of the series *Hawaii Five-O* immediately identified what distinguished the show from other dramas based on cops chasing criminals—it was set in America's 50th state. Filmed entirely on location for 12 years, starting in 1968, the show basked in the sunny, exotic, and picturesque beauty of the Hawaiian Islands. Otherwise, the longest continuous-running police drama in TV history featured a standard premise: a stern, cool investigator leading his partners in the methodical pursuit of underworld villains and diabolical maniacs.

Jack Lord starred as Steve McGarrett, the leader of a special Hawaii state police unit known as Five-O. McGarrett reported directly to Gov. Philip Grey (Richard Denning), but his team worked out of the Ionala Palace in downtown Honolulu. (The Palace had once been home to the Hawaiian legislature; in the five years prior to the series, it had become a museum.) The only glimpse viewers got of McGarrett's personal life was his enthusiasm for sailing, which he especially enjoyed after solving a case. Otherwise, the plots centered on the business of solving crimes and the terse interaction between McGarrett and his associates.

For 11 of *Hawaii Five-O*'s 12 seasons, James MacArthur portrayed McGarrett's top assistant, Danny "Dano" Williams. Kam Fong played Det. Chin Ho Kelly for 10 years but was killed off at the end of the 1978 season, and single-named Hawaiian actor Zulu was the massive Det. Kono Kalakaua. In the final year, McGarrett received a new string of assistants, and the ratings fell. In one of the final episodes, the inspector finally arrested his long-standing opponent, Wo Fat (Khigh Dhiegh).

Hawaii Five-O (CBS), 1968–1980. (original cast) Det. Steve McGarrett: Jack Lord, Det. Danny "Dano" Williams: James MacArthur (1968–1979), Det. Chin Ho Kelly: Kam Fong (1968–1978), Det. Kono Kalakaua: Zulu (1968–1972), Governor Philip Grey: Richard Denning.

Marcus Welby, M.D.

At age 62, actor Robert Young stepped out of retirement to accept the title role of the gentle, wise family practitioner in *Marcus Welby, M.D.* The doctor set up his office in a comfortable, converted house in Santa Monica, California, employing a fiery, young associate, Dr. Steven Kiley (James Brolin), and a caring, loyal nurse, Consuelo Lopez (Elena Verdugo).

Kiley had initially signed on for a one-year internship before pursuing neurology at a hospital, but Welby's virtues convinced him to stay with the practice. The two often clashed, usually because Kiley's academic, medical school approach to treatment differed from Welby's compassionate, by-the-gut reactions to his patients' needs. The kindly older

This picture captures well the warm, wholesome quality that made Marcus Welby, M.D. so popular. To the left is the doctor's nurse, Consuelo Lopez, played by Elena Verdugo. Guest star Belinda Montgomery is on the right and Young as the good doctor is center with his youthful patient of the moment.

doctor regularly discerned that the problem rested beyond the ailment, involving himself in his patients' lives with a psychiatric concern for their well-being.

Actress Anne Baxter originally appeared as Welby's romantic interest, but she disappeared after the first season. Sharon Gless arrived as second nurse Kathleen Faverty in 1974, and the next season

Kiley started dating Janet Blake (Pamela Hensley), the public relations director of a nearby hospital. The two married during a 1975 episode.

Marcus Welby, in its second year, became the first ABC series to rank as the most popular continuing show for a full season. The series ran for seven years, ending in 1975.

As a family practitioner, Marcus Welby (Robert Young, right) didn't have to don a surgical gown often. But he is seen here in the operating room with his young, headstrong associate, Dr. Steven Kiley, played by James Brolin.

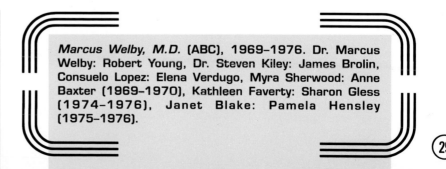

Marcus Welby, M.D. (ABC), 1969–1976. Dr. Marcus Welby: Robert Young, Dr. Steven Kiley: James Brolin, Consuelo Lopez: Elena Verdugo, Myra Sherwood: Anne Baxter (1969–1970), Kathleen Faverty: Sharon Gless (1974–1976), Janet Blake: Pamela Hensley (1975–1976).

Like his 20th-century counterpart, superspy James Bond, Secret Service agent James West (Robert Conrad) was always getting into seemingly escape-proof traps, such as the one pictured here.

The Wild, Wild West was essentially a fantasy Western. The hour-long CBS series premiered in 1965 with Robert Conrad as James T. West, who was part James Bond, part stylish Old West hero.

West was a specially trained Secret Service agent sent to the American frontier by President Ulysses S. Grant (James Gregory). His droll, heavy-set sidekick, Artemus Gordon (Ross Martin), was a master of disguises and dialects, and the daring duo traveled in a uniquely designed railroad car which stored an unusual arsenal of weapons and gadgets.

West, like the modern super-agent heroes on whom he was modeled, was a dashing figure, capable of fighting intimidating adversaries without mussing his hair or wrinkling his well-tailored western clothes. He continually encountered beautiful women and outrageously impossible situations. Gordon used his special talents to portray multiple characters, appearing as a drunken Portuguese fisherman one week, an arrogant German baron the next. Together, the duo relied on trickery, clever mechanical devices, and exotic weapons in their fight against fiendish adversaries, most of whom were madmen out to destroy the United States or egomaniacs bent on ruling the world. One villain—the evil dwarf genius, Dr. Miguelito Loveless (Michael Dunn)—proved to be a particularly cunning opponent who kept resurfacing.

The series was canceled in 1969 after four years.

The Wild, Wild West (CBS), 1965–1969. James T. West: Robert Conrad, Artemus Gordon: Ross Martin, Mr. Miguelito Loveless: Michael Dunn, Ulysses S. Grant: James Gregory.

Set improbably in cowpoke country, *The Wild, Wild West* featured Ross Martin (left) as Artemus Gordon, a master of disguises and dialects, and Robert Conrad as James West, the heroic federal agent working directly for President Ulysses S. Grant.

The Mod Squad united the 1960s youth culture with the tried-and-true television format of a police series. Premiering in 1968, the same year as the Chicago riots, the hour-long ABC series featured three rebellious dropouts from U.S. society—"hippies," that is—who were transformed into an undercover team after their individual run-ins with the law.

Pete Cochrane (Michael Cole) was an intense, shaggy-haired youth from a well-to-do Beverly Hills family who had stolen a car after getting kicked out of his home by his parents. Linc Hayes (Clarence Williams III), who grew up as one of 13 children in a ghetto in the Watts neighborhood of Los Angeles, was arrested while participating in the Watts riots. Julie Barnes (Peggy Lipton), the daughter of a San Francisco prostitute, was arrested for vagrancy in Los Angeles after running away from home.

The trio were on probation when Captain Adam Greer (Tige Andrews) tracked them down to recruit them for a special investigative squad. The unit was formed to penetrate the seamier side of the 1960s culture and to identify the sleazy shysters who traded on disaffected youth. The culprits, as it turned out, were invariably over 30 years of age.

In addition to the usual chase scenes and tense showdowns, the show centered on the argumentative trio, as they repeatedly debated their own values and actions and questioned the motives of their superiors. Despite their tentative natures, they always bagged the bad guys.

The show was canceled in 1973 after five seasons.

The Mod Squad

The Mod Squad (ABC), 1968–1973. Pete Cochrane: Michael Cole, Linc Hayes: Clarence Williams III, Julie Barnes: Peggy Lipton, Capt. Adam Greer: Tige Andrews.

I Spy

In an age of gadget-laden super-agents, Robert Culp (left) and Bill Cosby brought a refreshing level of reality and down-to-earth humor to their roles in I Spy.

I Spy focused on two American secret agents, a top-ranked tennis pro and his trainer, who traveled the world taking part in international tournaments. Robert Culp portrayed the tennis player, Kelly Robinson, a Princeton University law student who had competed on two Davis Cup teams. Bill Cosby, in the first starring role for an African-American in a dramatic series, played Alexander Scott, a Rhodes Scholar and Temple University graduate whose fluency in foreign languages often came in handy.

Producer Sheldon Leonard gambled in hiring stand-up comic Cosby for the role. Not only did he break the color barrier for a dramatic series, he impressively displayed his ability to handle dramatic material. Indeed, he won three consecutive Emmy awards for Outstanding Actor in a Continuing Drama Series.

I Spy deviated from the standard secret agent series. Instead of portraying James Bond-style heroes, capable of accomplishing the near-impossible time after time while conquering every pretty woman in sight, the show featured more or less average men, capable of laughing at themselves and their work. Though dedicated to government service and to their country, they maintained a casual approach to life. They also questioned their superiors and weren't above criticizing the motives behind their orders. The hour-long adventure series debuted on NBC in 1965 and lasted three seasons.

I Spy (NBC), 1965–1968. Kelly Robinson: Robert Culp, Alexander Scott: Bill Cosby.

When a gunman's bullet hit the spine of Robert Ironside (Raymond Burr) and paralyzed him from the waist down, it looked like the end of a distinguished 25-year career for the chief of detectives of the San Francisco Police Department. But the fictional Ironside convinced a police commissioner that his expertise and passion for investigative work could still be of help, and the veteran detective was given the title of special consultant to the force. Ironside moved into a formerly vacant office at police headquarters and then went about solving difficult cases despite the confines of a wheelchair.

Burr took the Ironside role in 1967, only one year after the nine-season run of *Perry Mason* came to an end. He brought to the city streets the same kind of sharp intelligence and droll humor that had marked his behavior in the courtroom. For assistance, he made good use of a specially equipped police van and an array of young officers, including members of his former staff, Lt. Ed Brown (Don Galloway) and policewoman Eve Whitfield (Barbara Anderson). An ex-juvenile delinquent, Mark Sanger (Don Mitchell), joined up as bodyguard while working his way through law school. Anderson left in 1971 over a contract dispute and was replaced by Elizabeth Baur as Fran Belding.

Ironside provided Burr with another long-running hit, one that consistently ranked among the Top 20 programs from 1968 to 1973. It was canceled in 1975.

Assisting Ironside with the sleuthing were Don Galloway (standing) as Lt. Ed Brown and Barbara Anderson as Officer Eve Whitfield. They don't look too happy with the answers their questions are producing in the investigation at hand.

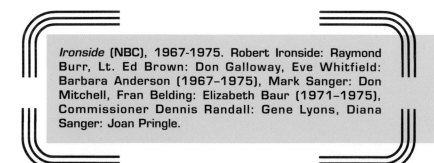

Ironside (NBC), 1967-1975. Robert Ironside: Raymond Burr, Lt. Ed Brown: Don Galloway, Eve Whitfield: Barbara Anderson (1967–1975), Mark Sanger: Don Mitchell, Fran Belding: Elizabeth Baur (1971–1975), Commissioner Dennis Randall: Gene Lyons, Diana Sanger: Joan Pringle.

Ironside

Fresh from his triumph as lawyer Perry Mason, Raymond Burr (right) portrayed Robert Ironside, the wheelchair-bound head of a special crime-solving unit attached to the San Francisco Police Department. His personal assistant, Mark Sanger, was played by Don Mitchell.

The three principal members of the *Star Trek* cast were (l. to r.) William Shatner as the young, somewhat impetuous Capt. James T. Kirk; DeForrest Kelley as the crusty ship's doctor, Leonard "Bones" McCoy; and Leonard Nimoy as the eminently logical, half-Vulcan–half-human Mr. Spock.

After decades of reruns and an ever-growing cult audience, it's hard to remember that *Star Trek* was not originally successful. In fact, in its three seasons on NBC, the show nevér rose above number 52 in the year-end program ratings. It only lasted as long as it did because after the second year a letter-writing campaign by young fans kept it alive for another season.

Set in the 23rd century, the science-fiction drama traced the adventures of the crew of the starship *Enterprise*, a spacecraft as large as an ocean liner which was capable of venturing through the galaxies. The ship and its crew had been commissioned by the United Federation of Planets "to seek out new life and new civilizations," as the introduction stated, and to deliver supplies to earth stations in space. The adventurers continually encountered alien cultures, some of them hostile, and repeatedly battled two other powerful races, the Romulans and the Klingons.

William Shatner starred as Capt. James T. Kirk, a forceful, impetuous leader. His top lieutenant had pointed ears, a green complexion, and a completely logical mind. Known as Mr. Spock (Leonard Nimoy), he was a cold, unemotional science officer whose father was a Vulcan ambassador and his mother an Earthling. Other regular cast members included an intense, sarcastic surgeon, Dr. Leonard "Bones" McCoy (DeForest Kelley); the impish, witty chief engineer, Montgomery "Scotty" Scott (James Doohan); the hard-working helmsman, Mr. Sulu (George Takei); and the communications officer, Lieutenant Uhura (Nichelle Nichols).

In 1979, 10 years after the series ceased production, all of the original cast members were reunited for a theatrical release entitled *Star Trek— The Motion Picture*. Since then, five more feature films have been produced.

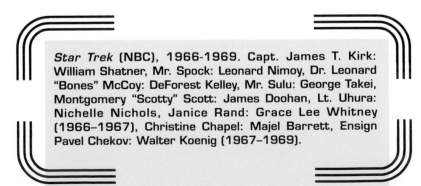

Star Trek (NBC), 1966-1969. Capt. James T. Kirk: William Shatner, Mr. Spock: Leonard Nimoy, Dr. Leonard "Bones" McCoy: DeForest Kelley, Mr. Sulu: George Takei, Montgomery "Scotty" Scott: James Doohan, Lt. Uhura: Nichelle Nichols, Janice Rand: Grace Lee Whitney (1966–1967), Christine Chapel: Majel Barrett, Ensign Pavel Chekov: Walter Koenig (1967–1969).

This is the starship *Enterprise*, whose mission was "to boldly go where no man has gone before."

Waiting to be "beamed down" are the other officers of the *Enterprise*: (l. to r.) Sulu played by George Takei, Uhura played by Nichelle Nichols, Pavel Chekov played by Walter Koenig, and Montgomery "Scotty" Scott, played by James Doohan.

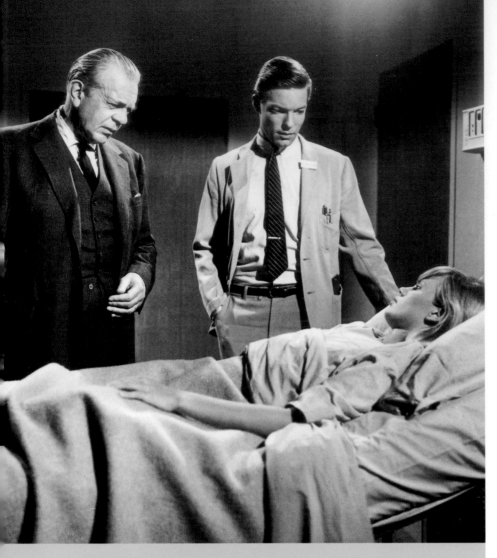

Richard Chamberlain (right) became a TV star playing James Kildare, the young, idealistic intern at Blair General Hospital. Kildare's supervisor and mentor, Dr. Gillespie (Raymond Massey), is at left.

Dr. Kildare

By the time ABC unveiled its prime-time series in 1961, the fictional Dr. James Kildare had survived several decades and various entertainment forms. He was introduced in the 1930s in a series of popular short stories written by Frederick Shiller Faust under his pen name, Max Brand. The plots, Faust later said, were inspired by urologist George Winthrop Fish.

In 1938, the first of several Dr. Kildare movies was released. The next year, a radio series began. Finally, NBC hired a young Richard Chamberlain to play the handsome, dedicated intern of Blair General Hospital in a weekly dramatic format for TV.

By coincidence, *Dr. Kildare* appeared in the same year as *Ben Casey*, ABC's series about another surgeon, older and more seasoned than Kildare. Both series quickly found large followings, lasted five years, and featured tense dramatizations of the life-and-death struggles found in large metropolitan hospitals. The difference between them lay in their depictions of the lead characters: as an intern, Kildare was idealistic and actively trying to learn about his profession, while the more taciturn Casey was a seasoned pro. The actors suited the temperaments of their characters. Chamberlain had a bright, eager countenance, where Vince Edwards as Casey rarely smiled.

A carry-over from Kildare's earlier incarnations was the wise but somewhat crusty Dr. Leonard Gillespie (Raymond Massey), whom Kildare met on a slightly more equal footing during the third season when he became a resident. In the program's fifth year, *Dr. Kildare* was split into two half-hour segments running on different days of the week. The series was canceled at the end of the season.

Dr. Kildare (NBC), 1961–1966. Dr. James Kildare: Richard Chamberlain, Dr. Leonard Gillespie: Raymond Massey, Dr. Simon Agurski: Eddie Ryder (1961–1962), Dr. Thomas Gerson: Jud Taylor (1961–1962), Receptionist Susan Deigh: Joan Patrick (1961–1962), Nurse Zoe Lawton: Lee Kurty (1965–1966).

Facing the bad guys was routine for private investigator Joe Mannix, played for eight seasons by Mike Connors. When the series started the detective was part of a high-tech agency but in the show's second year Mannix went off on his own.

Mannix was a bluntly titled program about a brawny, violence-prone detective, Joe Mannix. Mike Connors portrayed the manly hero with crisp, physical intensity. Nearly every program featured destructive car chases and savage, drawn-out fist fights, not to mention the occasional deadly shoot-out.

When the hour-long CBS series opened in 1967, Mannix was employed with the Los Angeles-based Intertect, a high-tech detective agency that used computers and scientific methods in its investigative efforts. Although Mannix employed the sophisticated devices, he just as often relied on intimidation and physical force.

By the second season, Mannix ventured out on his own, setting up a small, ground-floor office in the building where he resided. He was joined by his faithful, concerned secretary, Peggy Fair (Gail Fisher), whose late husband, a police officer killed on the job, had been Mannix's friend. His former Intertect boss, Lou Wickersham (Joseph Campanella), continued to appear during the second season but in the third year, he was replaced by Mannix's trusty police contact, Lt. Adam Tobias. Tobias was played by Robert Reed, who at the same time portrayed Mike Brady of *The Brady Bunch* on a rival network.

Receiving its highest ratings from 1970 to 1972, *Mannix* was canceled in 1975. During the series heyday, comedians Bob and Ray regularly parodied the program's premise with a skit called *Blimmix*.

Mannix (CBS), 1967–1975. Joe Mannix: Mike Connors, Lou Wickersham: Joseph Campanella (1967–1968), Peggy Fair: Gail Fisher (1968–1975), Lt. Adam Tobias: Robert Reed (1969–1975).

The Fugitive

While on the run, Kimble (Janssen, right) took odd jobs to support himself. This episode from September 1966 found him at an Indian school, where he encountered guest stars Hope Lange and Jaime Sanchez.

Mr. Richard Kimble (David Janssen) was a mistakenly marked man on the run from the law in the ABC series, *The Fugitive.* In the 1963 debut, the physician claimed that a one-armed man killed his wife, but only his sister, Donna (Jacqueline Scott), believed him. Instead, the doctor himself was accused of the murder, tried, convicted, and given the death sentence. Lt. Philip Gerard (Barry Morse) was escorting him to prison for his execution when their train derailed, knocking the officer unconscious and enabling Kimble to escape.

The fugitive set off in search of the one-armed killer (Bill Raisch). Meanwhile, Gerard, like Javert in *Les Misérables*, doggedly pursued the prisoner whom he had allowed to flee. For four seasons, Kimble tracked his prey, occasionally catching glimpses of him but never apprehending him. Likewise, Kimble regularly came close to capture but managed to slip away each time.

To support himself while on the run, he took on a series of odd jobs. These often brought him into contact with people whose lives briefly became entangled with his own.

In the final two episodes, the case was resolved. The one-armed man was arrested for another crime in Los Angeles, and Kimble surrendered. Then the true killer escaped. But the doctor convinced Gerard to let him join the hunt. He finally confronted his quarry in a showdown atop a water tower. Gerard arrived just in time to hear the killer confess, then shot the one-armed escapee to save the doctor's life.

The final show on August 29, 1967 drew a 72 percent share of the viewing audience, the largest number of people to tune in to a regular episode of a series until the "Who Shot J.R." cliff-hanger on *Dallas* in 1980.

From time to time during the series, Dr. Richard Kimble (David Janssen, right) wound up in the custody of his relentless pursuer, Lt. Philip Gerard (Barry Morse), but somehow the innocent fugitive always managed to escape.

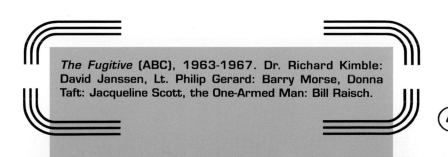

The Fugitive (ABC), 1963-1967. Dr. Richard Kimble: David Janssen, Lt. Philip Gerard: Barry Morse, Donna Taft: Jacqueline Scott, the One-Armed Man: Bill Raisch.

Millions of viewers vicariously enjoyed the no-ties experiences of Tod Stiles and Buzz Murdock (Martin Milner, left, and George Maharis) as they traveled one of America's major highways in a 1960 Corvette.

Route 66 followed the travels and travails of two spirited, rootless young men as they set out to see America in a 1960 Corvette. On the surface, the lead characters had little in common. Tod Stiles (Martin Milner) came from a wealthy family and attended Yale University, but when his father died suddenly he discovered that most of the family money was gone. Buzz Murdock (George Maharis) was a street-smart hustler who had learned to fend for himself while growing up in the tough Hell's Kitchen neighborhood of New York City. The two were connected through Murdock's employer, who was Stiles' father. When the older man died, Stiles and Murdock found themselves free to roam.

Filmed on location, the CBS series, which began in 1960, followed the duo as they aimlessly explored America from coast to coast. Their adventures resulted in romance, danger, intrigue, lessons about life, and comedy.

Maharis left the show in the middle of the 1962–1963 season because of a recurring bout of hepatitis. He continued to appear occasionally throughout the year, but was not a part of the following season. His replacement was Glenn Corbett as Lincoln "Linc" Case, a Vietnam war hero from Texas who was still recovering emotionally from his experiences in combat. He was ambivalent about his future, but interested in the sort of exploits that constant traveling presented. He and Stiles hooked up in March 1963 and remained traveling companions for the final season in 1963–1964.

Route 66

Route 66 (CBS), 1960-1964. Tod Stiles: Martin Milner, Buzz Murdock: George Maharis (1960–1963), Lincoln "Linc" Case: Glenn Corbett (1963–1964).

Children's Programming, Daytime Programming, and Game Shows

In 1961, after seven years on ABC, Walt Disney packed up Tinkerbell and the rest of his stable of cartoon characters, documentaries, and animals and transferred his television series to NBC. His new network allowed the future-minded Disney the chance to produce color telecasts for the first time, an opportunity that he cherished. His enthusiasm was evident in the program's new name: *Walt Disney's Wonderful World of Color*.

Disney crowned the inauguration of his NBC series with another jewel. On the September 24 debut, he introduced his first major new cartoon character in many years, the erudite Professor Ludwig von Drake, who was presented as the uncle of one of Disney's most famous animated creations, Donald Duck. The debut was entitled *An Adventure in Color: Mathmagic Land*, and it initiated a series of educational shows hosted by von Drake.

The debut of Disney's NBC show served to introduce the studio's first new cartoon character in many years, the erudite Professor Ludwig von Drake. He served as the host of the inaugural program and several others over the succeeding years.

 (Preceding page) One of the "stars" of <u>Sesame Street</u>—Big Bird.

The *Wonderful World of Color* seemed to inspire a new spurt of creativity in Disney, and the first few seasons of the show saw the production of several top-notch episodes, including a three-part "The Prince and the Pauper" a two-parter called "The Mooncussers," and the three-part "The Adventures of Gallagher." However, after Disney's death in 1966, the series relied increasingly on reruns of the studio's cartoons and movies.

In 1969, the show underwent another name change, becoming known as *The Wonderful World of Disney.* It was again retitled 10 years later, becoming *Disney's Wonderful World.* In 1981, the series moved to CBS, where it lasted two seasons.

With his two fascinated companions, the producer and on-air host of the Wonderful World of Color—Walt Disney himself—pores over a copy of Alice's Adventures in Wonderland and Through the Looking Glass. Disney's animated version of the Lewis Carroll stories premiered in 1951.

Walt Disney's Wonderful World of Color (NBC), 1961–1981; (CBS), 1981–1983. Host: Walt Disney (1961–1966).

Host Art Fleming readies contestants Helen, Joe, and Cris for Final Jeopardy, when they can bet all or part of their earnings on their written response to one question. The category of the day is the Gay 90s.

Jeopardy

Created by singer and talk show host Merv Griffin, *Jeopardy* developed into a classic game show by flipping the premise of the earliest quiz contests. Most game shows centered around a host who asked contestants questions and then waited for quick responses. *Jeopardy* provided a panel of three with the answers and expected them to come up with the right questions.

The game has followed the same format since its 1964 daytime premiere on NBC with Art Fleming as host. Three contestants face a game board consisting of six categories, and each category has five different answers hidden behind squares. A correct reply adds the amount named on the face of the square to the

contestant's winnings, and a wrong one subtracts that amount from the total. A second round doubles the amounts of each square. Then, in a third round known as "Final Jeopardy," the contestants can bet part or all of their winnings on their ability to pose the right question to one final answer. The person with the most money at the end returns for the next contest.

At a time when most game shows were growing simpler, *Jeopardy* posed difficult questions and tended to attract highly educated contestants. In 1974, the game show made a brief fling in prime time as a syndicated program, but it went off the air in 1975. However, it returned to NBC's daytime lineup for six months in 1978 and 1979. The show was revived again in 1984 as a syndicated program with a new host, Alex Trebek.

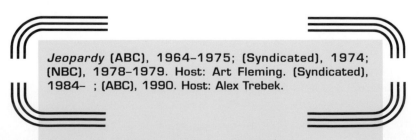

Jeopardy (ABC), 1964–1975; (Syndicated), 1974; (NBC), 1978–1979. Host: Art Fleming. (Syndicated), 1984– ; (ABC), 1990. Host: Alex Trebek.

Mister Rogers' Neighborhood

In the early 1950s, Fred Rogers, a Presbyterian minister from Pittsburgh, Pennsylvania, began using puppets and music to communicate with children. In 1955, he joined the cast of *The Children's Corner*, a Saturday morning series on NBC, and eight years later, he created his own children's show for Canadian television, calling it *MisteRogers' Neighborhood.* The 15-minute program ran until 1967, when the threat of cancellation produced major funding from Sears-Roebuck.

With his new support, Rogers changed the spelling of the show's title to *Mister Rogers' Neighborhood,* expanded to a 30-minute show five days a week, and joined the National Educational Television network (now PBS). The program was quickly picked up by most affiliates across the United States, and today, *Mister Rogers* ranks as the longest-running children's program on public TV.

What makes the show so special are the lessons and positive encouragement that Rogers gingerly offers children through the use of puppets, guests, stories, and low-key musical numbers. His primary goal, he has often said, is to make children feel good about themselves and to enable them to communicate their feelings. His daily topics have ranged from teaching children the meaning of the word "assassination" to showing youngsters how a household drain functions. Rogers also welcomes guests, most of them regulars like Mr. McFeely, "the Speedy Delivery Man." This sprightly old mail carrier is a dedicated show business buff who often breaks into tap dance steps.

The production of new *Mister Rogers* episodes ceased from 1975 to 1979. Then production resumed on a periodic basis. The series now combines some new episodes with reruns of older shows.

Mister Rogers' Neighborhood (PBS), 1967–1975; 1979– . Host: Fred Rogers.

Grayson Hall (center) played Dr. Julia Hoffman, who fell in love with Barnabas and dedicated herself to curing his vampirism. At right is Nancy Barrett as Carolyn Stoddard, the teen-age daughter of matriarch Elizabeth Collins Stoddard. Like other members of the cast, they also played their characters' 19th-century counterparts, seen here.

Dark Shadows

Dark Shadows put a sinister spin on the soap opera theme by combining characters from Gothic horror stories with the usual convoluted daytime tales of lust, romance, and tragedy. The ABC series, which ran in the late afternoons, attracting teens as well as housewives, created a stir with its premiere in 1966, drawing some initial protests about its romanticizing of evil in the delicate, after-school time period.

The series, situated in the eerie town of Collinsport, Maine, centered on the lives of the town's pioneering family, the Collinses, who lived in the creepy mansion, Collins House. Jonathan Frid starred as a handsome, 200-year-old vampire, Barnabas Collins, whose combination of elegance and evil proved enticing to the show's female fans. He led a cast of ghosts,

werewolves, and haunted spirits who called on the supernatural during the course of their daily lives. As soap operas go, Dark Shadows featured more action than romantic trauma, although unfaithful lovers and scheming, power-hungry community leaders were in evidence.

As the series progressed, the plots grew more adventurous, flashing between the 1800s and 1960s with dizzying regularity, thereby enabling actors with character counterparts in each century to create dual roles.

The series ended in 1971 after five seasons. In 1991, series creator Dan Curtis attempted to revive the show in prime time with Ben Cross as Barnabas, but the run was short-lived.

Dark Shadows (ABC), (1966–1971). Barnabas Collins: Jonathan Frid, Victoria Winters: Alexandra Moltke, Roger Collins: Louis Edmonds, David Collins: David Hennessy, Elizabeth Collins: Joan Bennett, Julia Hoffman: Grayson Hall, Quentin Collins: David Selby, Daphne Harridge: Kate Jackson, Angelique: Lara Parker, Reverend Trask: Jerry Lacy.

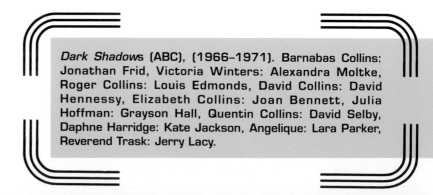

At the heart of the otherworldly doings in Dark Shadows was Jonathan Frid, who played the vampire, Barnabas Collins. Barnabas was the first of the undead to become a leading character in a daytime soap opera.

The Hollywood Squares

The Hollywood Squares united celebrities and the age-old competition of tic-tac-toe into a long-lasting game show. Premiering in 1966 with song-and-dance man Peter Marshall as the host, the show featured a set with a tri-level tic-tac-toe board. In each of the nine squares on the imposing structure sat a well-known individual from TV or the movies. The two contestants, who were designated as *O* or *X*, took turns selecting celebrities to answer questions put to them by Marshall. The contestant could then agree or disagree with the celebrity's answer. If he or she guessed correctly, that square was then marked accordingly, with an *X* or an *O*. If the contestant was wrong, the square was given to the opponent—unless it would provide the person with three squares in a row and a victory. He or she had to earn that for him- or herself. Each three-square triumph was credited to the winning contestant, and the one with the most rounds when time ran out won.

The game itself was simple. The popularity of *The Hollywood Squares* rested on the quips of the comical celebrities. Regular panelists over the years included Paul Lynde, Wally Cox, Charles Nelson Reilly, Carol Channing, Cliff Arquette (as Charley Weaver), Rose Marie, George Gobel, Rich Little, and Joan Rivers.

The Hollywood Squares was briefly shown in prime time in the spring of 1966 and the summer of 1967, with Marshall as host. A syndicated version, also with Marshall, was often shown at night. Both the NBC daytime show and the syndicated version were canceled in 1980. A new syndicated *The Hollywood Squares* with John Davidson as host began in 1986.

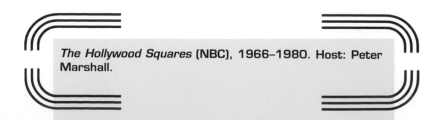

The Hollywood Squares (NBC), 1966–1980. Host: Peter Marshall.

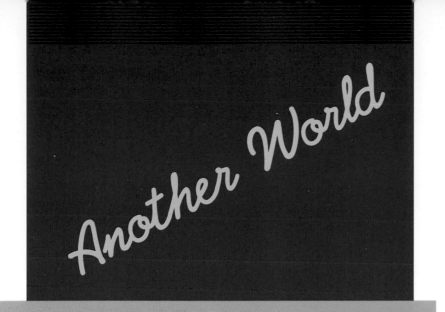

Another World

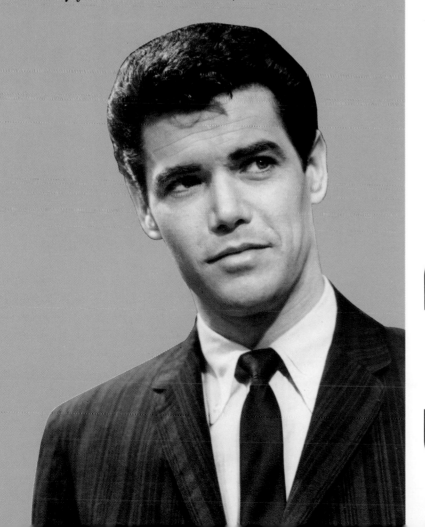

The last successful soap created by the prolific Irna Phillips, Another World focused on the trials and tribulations of the Matthews family. Joe Gallison, pictured here, played Bill Matthews, whose father, the head of an accounting firm, died as the series opened.

Another World was the last successful soap opera created by the prolific writer, Irna Phillips, who had helped set the tone for TV's melodramas with *As the World Turns* and *The Guiding Light*, two of the medium's most successful daytime programs.

Another World, which began on NBC in May 1964, was a huge daytime hit, one that also set a few precedents. It was the first soap to expand to an hour (in January 1975) and the first to run regularly for 90 minutes (from March 1979 to August 1980). It also was the first daytime drama to generate a spinoff: *Somerset* in 1970, then *Texas* in 1980.

With *Another World* Phillips created what she described as a psychological drama, emphasizing her characters' inner feelings and dreams and the major and minor events of their lives. Set in Bay City, the series originally concentrated on the Matthews family. Jim Matthews was an accountant, husband, and father of three who, over time, was played by John Beal, Leon Janney, Shepperd Strudwick, and Hugh Marlowe. His wife, Mary, was played by Virginia Dwyer. As the show progressed, it tracked the complex adult lives of the Matthews' children, Pat, Russ, and Alice, as well as those of Jim's widowed sister-in-law, Liz Matthews, and her children, Bill, Janet, and Susan. By the end of the 1970s, Jim and Mary Matthews had been written out of the series completely, with their children's extensive list of relatives, ex-lovers, and business associates taking center stage.

Among the actors to graduate to greater fame after stints on *Another World* were Ray Liotta, Audra Lindley, Ann Wedgeworth, Faith Ford, Kyra Sedgwick, and Dack Rambo.

Another World (NBC), 1964– . Jim Matthews: John Beal; Leon Janney; Shepperd Strudwick; Hugh Marlowe, Mary Matthews: Virginia Dwyer, Pat Matthews: Susan Trustman; Beverly Penberthy, Dr. Russ Matthews: Joey Trent; Sam Groom; Bob Hover; David Bailey, Alice Matthews: Jacqueline Courtney; Susan Harney; Wesley Ann Pfenning; Vana Tribbey; Linda Borgeson, Liz Matthews: Sara Cunningham; Audra Lindley; Nancy Wickwire; Irene Dailey, Bill Matthews: Joe Gallison, Janet Matthews: Liza Chapman, Susan Matthews: Fran Sharon; Roni Dengel; Lisa Cameron; Lynn Milgrim.

Sesame Street

In 1967, Joan Ganz Cooney established the Children's Television Workshop with the intention of creating a daily educational program for youngsters. To underwrite the venture, she gathered financial support from the U.S. Office of Education, the Carnegie Corporation, and the Ford Foundation, and in 1969, the National Educational Television Network (now PBS) introduced her program, *Sesame Street*, to America.

In addition to Jim Henson's Muppets, Sesame Street featured live actors. The adult regulars seen here are (l. to r.) Mr. Hooper (Will Lee), Gordon (Matt Robinson), Susan (Loretta Long), and Bob (Bob McGrath).

Sesame Street was targeted specifically at the children of America's inner cities. Thus, the program is set on a city thoroughfare and features a multiethnic, multicultural cast. Nevertheless, the show quickly caught on with youngsters from all walks of life and all regions of the country.

Using a progressive, quick-cut style of production, drawn primarily from TV commercials, *Sesame Street* revolutionized children's television and set a new standard for creative ways to teach numbers, letters, and beginning grammar to youngsters. Along the way, the program, which uses skits, songs, animation, and puppetry to present lessons, introduced the artistry of Jim Henson's Muppets to a national audience. These expressive puppets, who star alongside good-natured adult cast members, immediately established a strong connection with their viewers. The memorable Muppet cast includes the Cookie Monster, Oscar the Grouch, Ernie, Bert, Kermit the Frog, Miss Piggy, Grover, and

Big Bird (the latter was not a puppet, but a life-size figure played by Henson associate Frank Oz).

The program remains a staple of the afternoon lineup of public television today.

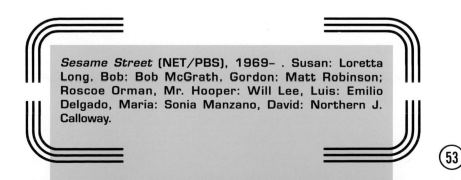

Sesame Street (NET/PBS), 1969– . Susan: Loretta Long, Bob: Bob McGrath, Gordon: Matt Robinson; Roscoe Orman, Mr. Hooper: Will Lee, Luis: Emilio Delgado, Maria: Sonia Manzano, David: Northern J. Calloway.

All one had to do to bargain for valuable prizes on Let's Make a Deal was dress in outlandish costumes, scream and shout to get dealmaster Monty Hall's attention, and otherwise be willing to make a complete fool of oneself in front of millions of viewers.

no skills, and no mental or physical dexterity. It did, however, encourage contestants to act as loud and silly as possible, and it required that they bring something ridiculous to trade for a chance to win prizes.

Co-produced and developed by host Monty Hall, *Let's Make a Deal* first appeared as a daily afternoon show on NBC in 1963 and was an instant hit. Each weekday, 31 contestants were invited from the studio audience to step into a "trading area." Then Hall, "TV's big dealer," would walk up and down the elevated aisles as the contestants screamed for his attention and the chance to play.

If chosen, the participant was given a choice between two prizes: usually, one prize was displayed while another was hidden behind a box, behind a door, or in a wallet. Sometimes the secret prize was more lucrative, sometimes it was worthless—the latter items were known as "zonks." If a contestant won a nice prize, he or she was often enticed to trade it in for another hidden opportunity, which was, again, sometimes worthless. At the end of the show, the two biggest winners were offered the chance to trade for "the big deal of the day." Each contestant could choose from among three doors, with one featuring more than $10,000 in prizes, and the others significantly lesser amounts.

Let's Make a Deal ran daily for five years on NBC and another eight on ABC. In 1967, NBC featured it in prime time as a summer replacement show, then ABC featured a weekly nighttime version from 1969 to 1971.

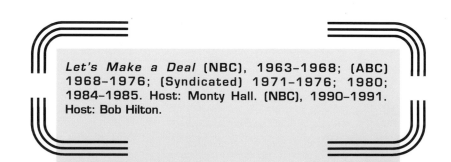

Let's Make a Deal (NBC), 1963–1968; (ABC) 1968–1976; (Syndicated) 1971–1976; 1980; 1984–1985. Host: Monty Hall. (NBC), 1990–1991. Host: Bob Hilton.

The game show *Let's Make a Deal* traded on the willingness of average people to dress in outrageous costumes for the opportunity to win prizes and cash. The competition required no knowledgeable answers,

News, Sports, and Special Events

In 1960, Broadway's acclaimed musical star, Mary Martin, brought her interpretation of the boy-who-wouldn't-grow-up to television for the third time. Unlike the previous live versions, this airing was taped.

(Preceding page) Walter Cronkite, the anchor of *The CBS Evening News* from 1962 to 1981.

Peter Pan

In 1960, NBC decided to broadcast Mary Martin's popular musical version of *Peter Pan* in a lavish, taped adaptation designed to show off the network's advanced color capabilities (and perhaps sell more sets for the parent company, RCA).

It wasn't the first time that the veteran Broadway actress had brought the children's classic to TV. A live version had aired on *Producer's Showcase* in March 1955, attracting a huge audience and critical raves. The show was restaged for another live broadcast in January 1956. By the time of the 1960 version, critics were warning that the new adaptation might tarnish the success of the previous productions. Some questioned the choice to again feature Mary Martin in the lead role and Cyril Ritchard as Captain Hook.

However, when the show aired, the critics raved. The revival, said the *New York Times*, "didn't affect the radiant delicacy and impish gusto" of the story and its main character. Based on a 1904 tale by James M. Barrie, *Peter Pan* relates the adventures of the three youngsters of the proper British Darling family, each of whom boasts a great imagination. One night, an elfin boy in green tights named Peter Pan appears. He teaches the children to fly and whisks them away to Never-Never Land, where they encounter fairies, Indians, and pirates. The latter are led by the infamous Captain Hook.

The triumphant special was adapted and choreographed by Jerome Robbins and directed by Vincent Donehue. The lyrics were by Carolyn Leigh, Betty Comden, and Adolph Green and the music was by Moose Charlap and Jules Styne. Because it was taped, the 1960 version of *Peter Pan* has been preserved for new generations of youngsters to enjoy on videocassette.

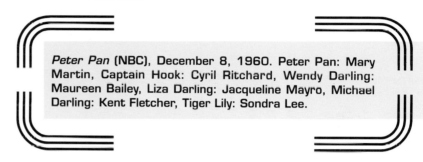

Peter Pan (NBC), December 8, 1960. Peter Pan: Mary Martin, Captain Hook: Cyril Ritchard, Wendy Darling: Maureen Bailey, Liza Darling: Jacqueline Mayro, Michael Darling: Kent Fletcher, Tiger Lily: Sondra Lee.

As on Broadway and in the live 1950s TV outings, Cyril Ritchard co-starred with Martin as Captain Hook, the pirate who liked to think of himself as the "slimiest rat in the pack."

Pictured here are the correspondents who carried 60 Minutes to its initial burst of widespread popularity—(l. to r.) Dan Rather, Morley Safer, and Mike Wallace. Only Wallace has been with the weekly newsmagazine since its inception.

60 Minutes

Billed as a weekly televised newsmagazine, *60 Minutes* ranks just behind *The Tonight Show* and *Walt Disney* as television's longest-running evening program. The series premiered in 1968, originally alternating with *CBS Reports*. Instead of focusing on one topic an hour, as *Reports* did, *60 Minutes* allowed for shorter features, blending hard-hitting investigative exposes, in-depth news stories, and lighter features on American culture and celebrities.

In 1971, the series moved to Sunday evenings, but it was often pre-empted by live football coverage. Finally, starting in 1975, it matured into a weekly telecast that aired no matter how long the games ran.

The format has remained relatively stable over the years. Each program opens with the ticking of a large stop watch, followed by previews of the night's stories framed by a mock magazine cover. Two to three features then follow, with the ticking stop watch reappearing between segments to let viewers know how much time remains in the program.

For the first two seasons, the show was co-hosted by news veterans Mike Wallace and Harry Reasoner. In 1970, Reasoner went to ABC and was replaced by Morley Safer, a former CBS foreign bureau chief. Five years later, former CBS White House correspondent Dan Rather became the third member of the team. Since then, a number of changes in on-camera personnel have taken place, including Reasoner's return to the show in 1978; Rather's departure in 1981 to become the anchor of *The CBS Evening News* and his replacement by Ed Bradley; and the addition of a woman, Diane Sawyer, who began a five-year stint on the show in 1984.

Unlike most programs, *60 Minutes* has grown more popular as the years have passed. It ended the 1979–1980 season as the top-rated prime-time series on the air and has remained near the top of the yearly rankings ever since.

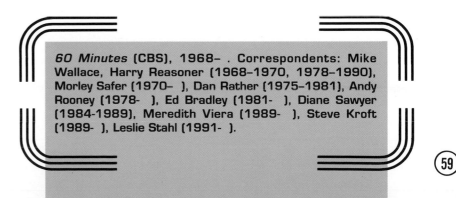

60 Minutes (CBS), 1968– . Correspondents: Mike Wallace, Harry Reasoner (1968–1970, 1978–1990), Morley Safer (1970–), Dan Rather (1975–1981), Andy Rooney (1978–), Ed Bradley (1981-), Diane Sawyer (1984-1989), Meredith Viera (1989–), Steve Kroft (1989-), Leslie Stahl (1991-).

Before the debate, the opponents shook hands. John F. Kennedy, the Democratic candidate (left), and Richard M. Nixon, the Republican candidate, were junior senators together and maintained a cordial relationship.

The First Nixon-Kennedy Debate

When Richard Nixon and John Kennedy squared off in the first nationally televised debate between two presidential candidates, Nixon was perceived as the front runner. He had been a highly visible vice-president for eight years alongside a popular president, Dwight D. Eisenhower, and had gained widespread attention when Ike suffered two heart attacks during his administration. Kennedy, by contrast, was a junior U.S. senator from Massachusetts with little name recognition outside of New England. As for the debate itself, Nixon was given the edge because he had had more experience in national campaigns and in front of a camera. With his famous "Checkers" speech in 1952, which saved his vice-presidential candidacy, he had also demonstrated his ability to use television to successfully manipulate public opinion, becoming, in fact, the first national politician to do so.

However, it wasn't the political veteran who came out on top on September 26, 1960. It was the charismatic Democrat. Indeed, political commentators trace the turning point in Kennedy's triumphant campaign to the first of the four nationally televised meetings between the two candidates. In fact, Kennedy's presentation in what are now known as the Great Debates may have been the deciding factor in one of the closest presidential elections in U.S. history.

The debate was held at the CBS-affiliated station, WBBM-TV, in Chicago. CBS produced the program, with Howard K. Smith as moderator. The candidates spoke for eight minutes each on domestic policy, then fielded questions for 35 minutes from a panel of broadcast journalists: Sander Vanocur of NBC, Robert Fleming of ABC, Stuart Novins of CBS, and Charles Warren of Mutual Broadcasting.

Before an estimated audience of 60 to 75 million people, the candidates were earnest, polite, and focused on the issues. Kennedy was seen as forceful, composed, articulate, and attractive. Nixon, however, seemed uncomfortable and defensive, dabbing his chin to wipe away the perspiration that emerged under the hot studio lights. Moreover, the vice-president looked wan, the result of his hospitalization for a knee injury just prior to the debate, and he wore a light-colored suit, which blended into the background of the set. By contrast, Kennedy, who was dressed in a dark suit, looked tan and fit.

Interestingly, those who listened on radio gave the debate to Nixon. But TV viewers saw the outcome the other way. For that reason, the debate was widely perceived as a turning point for American politics. It was the moment when the power of television forever changed the content and style of presidential campaigns by accentuating the importance of visual image and personal charisma.

The First Nixon-Kennedy Debate (all networks), September 26, 1960. Candidates: Richard M. Nixon, John F. Kennedy, Moderator: Howard K. Smith (CBS), Panelists: Sander Vanocur (NBC), Robert Fleming (ABC), Stuart Novins (CBS), Charles Warren (Mutual).

At the outset of the debate, moderator Howard K. Smith (center) introduced the candidates. Clearly evident in this photo is the degree to which Nixon's light suit blended into the background of the set. Also compare the vice-president's rather rigid posture with Kennedy's more relaxed demeanor.

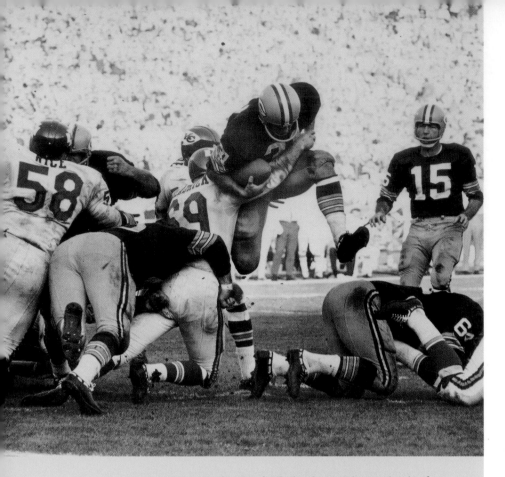

Running back Jimmy Taylor (#31) plows through the line to score for Green Bay, helping to take the Packers to their 35-10 victory over the Chiefs in Super Bowl I. The game's MVP, quarterback Bart Starr (#15), is at right.

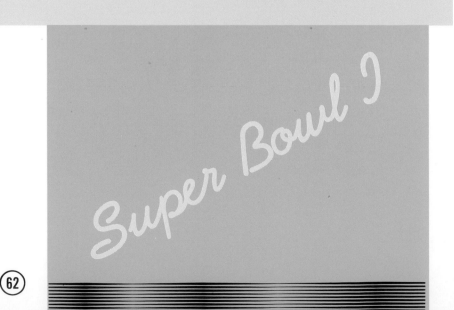

Super Bowl I

January 15, 1967 not only marked the first time the championship team from the upstart American Football League went head to head against the champs from the well-established National Football League. It was also the first time the same football contest was telecast simultaneously by CBS and NBC.

CBS owned a contract giving it the rights to telecast NFL games. NBC held a similar agreement with the AFL. That day, the biggest audience ever for a sports contest tuned in, but the 70 million fans were split between the two networks, with CBS garnering a slightly larger percentage.

A big part of the competition, at least for the networks, took place in the days prior to the game. CBS touted that its announcers included a one-time football star, Frank Gifford. NBC extolled the analytical ability and vast knowledge of its broadcast booth experts, Curt Gowdy and Paul Christman. On the day itself, NBC offered a pre-game special with in-depth looks at the players and the histories of the two leagues. CBS, meanwhile, led off with a basketball exhibition featuring the highly popular Harlem Globetrotters.

The game between the NFL's Green Bay Packers and the AFL's Kansas City Chiefs took place in sunny Los Angeles' Memorial Coliseum, with kick-off at 3:30 p.m. EST. It was a ho-hum affair. The NFL was still a dominant league and its players were stronger and more experienced. The Packers won 35-10.

The contest's name, by the way, was created by Chiefs' owner Lamar Hunt. He was among the many individuals trying to think of a catchy handle for the game when he overheard his children talking about a "Super Ball," the handball-sized rubber sphere that could bounce 10 times as high as a tennis ball. The title popped into his head at that moment, he later said.

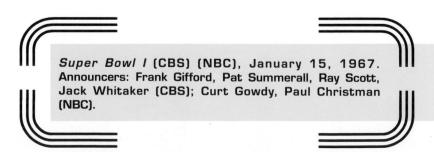

Super Bowl I (CBS) (NBC), January 15, 1967. Announcers: Frank Gifford, Pat Summerall, Ray Scott, Jack Whitaker (CBS); Curt Gowdy, Paul Christman (NBC).

The CBS Evening News with Walter Cronkite

Walter Cronkite took over the news anchor's chair from Douglas Edwards in April 1962. By 1974, Americans considered "Uncle Walter" the most trusted man in the nation.

In April 1962, when veteran broadcast journalist Walter Cronkite succeeded Douglas Edwards as the anchor for *The CBS Evening News*, NBC's rival *Huntley-Brinkley Report* was firmly entrenched as television's top-rated evening news program. With Cronkite at the helm, CBS gradually encroached on NBC's lead until by the end of the decade the former had taken over as the airwaves' number one newscast. Moreover, a 1974 poll found Cronkite to be the most trusted man in the United States. This distinction would have been impressive at any time, but it was particularly noteworthy during the Watergate era, when many Americans were rapidly losing faith in the institutions that they had once considered sacred.

Cronkite spoke with the self-assured naturalness of a seasoned communicator, and his clear, concise, soft-spoken style conveyed honesty and concern. He placed great value on objectivity. For instance, whenever Eric Sevareid closed the newscast with a commentary, Cronkite intentionally omitted his trademark sign-off, "And that's the way it is . . ."

Cronkite had joined United Press International in 1939 following a stint at a Kansas City radio station. After tracking Gen. Dwight Eisenhower across Europe during World War II, he emerged as one of the radio service's top reporters. Then, after the war, he served as a correspondent in Moscow. Finally, in 1950, when television was in its infancy, he joined CBS. Initially, he anchored the news at the Washington affiliate. Then, in 1952, he served as the anchor at the Democratic and Republican conventions. Throughout the 1950s, he also hosted several of CBS's public affairs programs and news documentary specials.

Cronkite, who also served as managing editor of *The CBS Evening News*, saw the newscast through several important developments, including its expansion from 15 to 30 minutes in September 1963 and its first color telecast in early 1966. He was also the first anchor to publicly state as fact that the American public had been misled by its government during the Vietnam war. Cronkite left the show on March 6, 1981. After nearly two decades as a newscaster, he was considered an American institution.

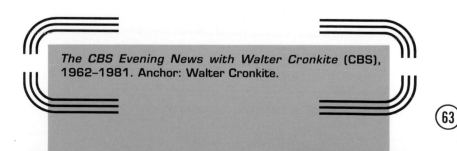

The CBS Evening News with Walter Cronkite (CBS), 1962–1981. Anchor: Walter Cronkite.

The Apollo XI Moon Landing

The networks had tracked the first voyage to the moon with heightened interest, starting with the roar of the lift-off. Regular coverage continued through the following four days, as three American astronauts—Neil Armstrong, Buzz Aldrin, and Michael Collins—hurtled through space aboard Apollo XI. Then, on July

20, 1969, Armstrong and Aldrin boarded the *Eagle* lunar module, detached from the primary craft, and headed toward the moon's surface. Shortly after 6 p.m. EST, more than 100 million Americans heard Armstrong report, "Houston, tranquility base here. The *Eagle* has landed."

It was high drama. But the networks had a problem. NASA had informed them that the astronauts would take a six-hour nap after landing. To the news' executives dismay, this meant that the moonwalk wouldn't start until two hours after midnight, after prime time was over. Nevertheless, the networks decided to cancel their regular evening programming and, instead, to broadcast live fare involving the space mission.

As it turned out, the astronauts decided to dispense with their naps upon landing. They were simply too keyed up to sleep. But it took them four hours—two longer than expected—to de-pressurize the cabin and open the *Eagle*'s door. Still, the outcome was well worth the wait. People all over the world watched in awe as Neil Armstrong slowly descended the ladder and stopped briefly at the bottom step. At 10:56 p.m. EST, he put his feet on the moon, saying "That's one small step for a man and one giant leap for mankind."

The networks stayed tuned as Armstrong took four backward steps, kicking the powdery surface to test its texture and depth. Aldrin joined him, and the two collected rocks, erected a U.S. flag, accepted a long-distance call from President Richard M. Nixon, and set up scientific equipment. In total, the men spent two-and-a-half hours on the moon's surface, attracting in the process the largest worldwide viewing audience in history.

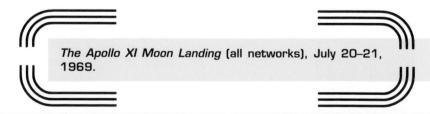

The Apollo XI Moon Landing (all networks), July 20–21, 1969.

Neil Armstrong took this photo of Buzz Aldrin descending the lunar module for his walk on the moon. The astronauts spent a total of two-and-a-half hours on the craggy surface.

The noon hour of November 22, 1963 found President Kennedy in an open limousine, following a parade route through the streets of Dallas, Texas. As seen here, his wife, Jacqueline, was beside him, but Texas governor John Connelly, next to Jackie, had moved into the front seat, ahead of Kennedy, by the time the car reached the Texas School Book Depository.

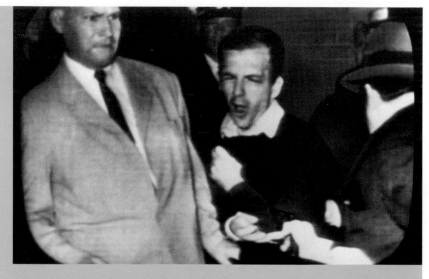

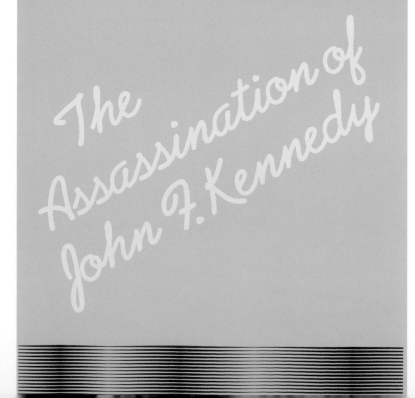

Viewers watching NBC at 12:20 p.m. on November 24 saw the live murder of alleged presidential assassin Lee Harvey Oswald by a Dallas nightclub owner, Jack Ruby. "There is absolute pandemonium," reported the on-the-spot correspondent, Tom Petit.

The Assassination of John F. Kennedy

In the early afternoon of November 22, 1963, CBS was airing a soap opera. NBC and ABC weren't on network time, so affiliates around the country were running local or syndicated programs. All three networks cut into the audio portions of their programming to announce that shots had been fired in Dallas in the vicinity of President John F. Kennedy's motorcade, and that someone in the car had been shot.

All three networks immediately switched to their national news studios for ongoing updates. CBS, with Dan Rather as the regional reporter in Dallas, was the first to carry an unconfirmed report of Kennedy's death. NBC refused to air the news until it was confirmed and was therefore the last network to make the announcement.

For four days, the three networks canceled all programming and commercials, offering nonstop reporting on the tragedy and subsequent news developments. The stations showed the arrest of Lee Harvey Oswald, the shell of Air Force One as Lyndon Johnson read the oath of office inside, a short press conference with Oswald at Dallas police headquarters, and the line of mourners as they filed past Kennedy's casket in the rotunda of the U.S. Capitol.

Only NBC was offering live footage of Oswald's prison transfer in Dallas on November 24 at 12:20 p.m., when Jack Ruby fatally gunned down the alleged presidential assassin before millions of viewers. Reporter Tom Petit, who was providing a voice-over when it happened, shouted, "He's been shot! He's been shot! Lee Harvey Oswald has been shot! There is absolute pandemonium . . ."

Overall, NBC presented 71 hours of news coverage that weekend. ABC aired 60, and CBS 55. An editorial by the *New York Times* suggested that television's coverage had united the country, and Congress passed a resolution commending the networks for their work.

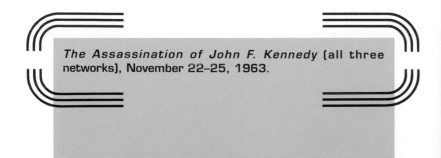

The Assassination of John F. Kennedy (all three networks), November 22–25, 1963.

On Monday, November 25, millions of Americans watched on television as the president's widow and two young children, Caroline (left) and John-John, paid their last respects to the assassinated chief executive.

ABC's Wide World of Sports

Long before cable's ESPN network, *ABC's Wide World of Sports* proved that American television viewers hungered for more than coverage of such conventional sports as baseball, football, and basketball. *Wide World of Sports* covered anything and everything that could remotely be labeled a sport—from arm wrestling to cliff diving to a demolition derby—and people tuned in by the masses.

Wide World of Sports, the brainchild of ABC executive Roone Arledge, premiered in 1961, filling Saturday afternoons with competitive activities from around the world. The initial telecast featured the series' now-famous introduction concerning "the thrill of victory and the agony of defeat," accompanied by the spectacular tumble taken by Yugoslavian Vinko Bogataj during a ski jump.

From the beginning, the show delved into the human element of sports, featuring stories that were "up close and personal," to use another famous slogan created by Arledge. These segments personalized competitors by introducing viewers to their personalities, their families, and their hometowns. Thus, when it came time for the competition, audiences had established a bond with the individuals whose achievements—and disappointments—they viewed.

Jim McKay, a one-time quiz show emcee, has won several Emmy awards as the host of the series. Other commentators over the years have included Keith Jackson, Chris Schenkel, Howard Cosell, Frank Gifford, Bud Palmer, and Bill Flemming. The show's popularity led to an expansion to Sunday afternoons in the 1970s and early 1980s.

Emmy-Award-winning Jim McKay has been the host of ABC's Wide World of Sports since the program's inception. Thanks to the show's wide-ranging approach, he has perhaps logged more miles and covered a broader range of sports than any other commentator in TV history.

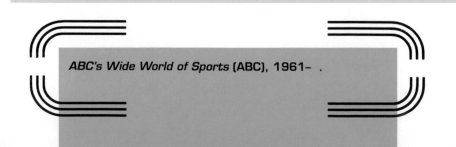

ABC's Wide World of Sports (ABC), 1961– .

Situation Comedies

(Preceding page) Three of the leads in <u>Hogan's Heroes</u> were (l. to r.) John Banner as Sgt. Hans Schultz, Bob Crane as Col. Robert Hogan, and Werner Klemperer as Col. Klink.

When <u>My Three Sons</u> premiered in 1960, the cast of regulars included (rear l. to r.) William Frawley as Bub, Tim Considine as Mike, (front l. to r.) Stanley Livingston as Chip, Fred MacMurray as Steve, and Don Grady as Robbie.

My Three Sons

In 1960, after several decades as a major film star, Fred MacMurray settled into his most famous role as the infinitely patient Steve Douglas, a widower who presided over his family of youngsters on *My Three Sons*. Although Douglas was an aerodynamics engineer, he seemed to spend most of his time providing a calming presence to the three rambunctious boys as they weathered puberty, dating, school, sports, camping trips, and other adventures.

The stable Douglas household also grew increasingly transitory as time passed. When the 30-minute series premiered on ABC, the family included 18-year-old Mike (Tim Considine), 14-year-old Robbie (Don Grady), and seven-year-old Chip (Stanley Livingston). Helping with the chores was Steve's father-in-law, cantankerous Bub O'Casey (William Frawley).

In 1965, the series moved to CBS. Cranky Uncle Charley O'Casey (William Demarest) joined the clan, replacing Frawley, who had died near the end of the previous season. Considine had outgrown his role, so Mike married his long-time girlfriend, Sally Morrison (Meredith MacRae), and left the show under the guise of moving east to teach college. To keep the program's name intact, Steve adopted an orphan, Ernie (Barry Livingston, real-life brother of Stanley).

In 1967, the family moved west because of Steve's work. Robbie married and had triplets—his three sons. Steve wedded one of Ernie's teachers, the widow Barbara Harper (Beverly Garland). Chip married in 1970, and the clan grew increasingly fragmented, with episodes often based on the interaction among only part of the family.

Although the enduring series was still ranked among TV's Top 20 in its eleventh season, it was canceled in 1972, after 12 years on the air.

My Three Sons (ABC), 1960–1965; (CBS), 1965–1972. Steve Douglas: Fred MacMurray, Mike Douglas: Tim Considine (1960–1965), Robbie Douglas: Don Grady, Chip Douglas: Stanley Livingston, Bub O'Casey: William Frawley (1960–1964), Charley O'Casey: William Demarest (1965–1972), Ernie Thompson Douglas: Barry Livingston (1963–1972), Sally Morrison: Meredith MacRae (1963–1965), Katie Miller: Tina Cole (1967–1972), Barbara Harper: Beverly Garland (1969–1972), Polly Williams: Ronnie Troup (1970–1972).

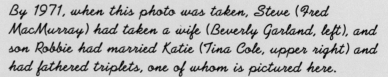

By 1971, when this photo was taken, Steve (Fred MacMurray) had taken a wife (Beverly Garland, left), and son Robbie had married Katie (Tina Cole, upper right) and had fathered triplets, one of whom is pictured here.

In the first situation comedy to feature an African-American woman who wasn't a domestic, *Julia* starred Diahann Carroll as a nurse at a Los Angeles aerospace firm. Her boss, Dr. Morton Chegley, was played by Lloyd Nolan.

Julia

Diahann Carroll was a singer who had starred in the Richard Rodgers musical, *No Strings*, on Broadway prior to her first major television role as the young widow, Julia Baker, in *Julia*. When the 30-minute series premiered on NBC in 1968, it marked the first time that a black woman had played the lead in a situation comedy since 1953. And, unlike the earlier instance, *Beulah*, the lead in *Julia* was not a domestic servant.

The series focused on Baker's struggles as a career woman and a single mother. Her husband, an Air Force captain, had been killed in combat in Vietnam, leaving her to raise six-year-old Corey (Marc Copage) by herself. To pick up the pieces of her life, she took a job as a nurse at an aerospace firm in Los Angeles. Her boss was crusty Dr. Morton Chegley (Lloyd Nolan), a demanding old-timer whose occasional belligerence was balanced by a warm heart. Baker also found a friend in chief nurse Hannah Yarby (Lurene Tuttle). The show followed Julia as she gained inner strength and independence.

At home, Baker lived in a modern, integrated apartment, where the show focused on her rather normal life: her son's best friend was a white neighbor, Earl J. Waggedorn (Michael Link), and she was courted first by Paul Cameron (Paul Winfield) and then by Steve Bruce (Fred Williamson). The show attracted viewers from all segments and regions of American society, remaining on the air for three seasons.

Julia (NBC), 1968–1971. Julia Baker: Diahann Carroll, Dr. Morton Chegley: Lloyd Nolan, Corey Baker: Marc Copage, Hannah Yarby: Lurene Tuttle (1968–1970), Earl J. Waggedorn: Michael Link, Marie Waggedorn: Betty Beaird, Leonard Waggedorn: Hank Brandt, Melba Chegley: Mary Wickes, Sol Cooper: Ned Glass, Paul Cameron: Paul Winfield (1968–1971), Steve Bruce: Fred Williamson (1970–1971).

Julia (Carroll) was a single mother trying to raise her six-year-old son (Marc Copage) by herself. In 1968, when the show premiered, that was an adventurous premise for a sitcom.

Why fold laundry when all you have to do is raise your arm and twitch your nose? Still, Samantha Stevens (Elizabeth Montgomery) tried to play it straight most of the time.

Bewitched

For the first five years of the show's run, Samantha's beleaguered husband, a hard-working advertising account executive named Darin, was played by Dick York, seen here in a shot from the series' premiere season.

Bewitched traced the amusing experiences of an attractive young witch as she attempted to repress her supernatural powers to please her loving but eternally exasperated husband.

The 30-minute ABC series, which premiered in 1964, starred Elizabeth Montgomery, who brought a sparkling intelligence to the role of Samantha Stevens. For five seasons, Dick York portrayed her mortal husband, hard-working advertising account executive Darin Stevens. Dick Sargeant took over the role in 1969.

Try as she might, Samantha kept finding compelling reasons to use her witchly abilities, needing only to twitch her nose to bring them into play. In this, she was constantly encouraged by her mischievous relatives: her mother, Endora (Agnes Moorehead); her father, Maurice (Maurice Evans); her forgetful Aunt Clara (Marion Lorne); and her Uncle Arthur (Paul Lynde). In later years, Montgomery doubled as her naughty look-alike cousin, Serena.

Samantha's exploits repeatedly caused problems for her husband, especially at work with his meddling boss, Larry Tate (David White), and with the Stevens' nosy neighbors, the Kravitzes. In later years, Darin's problems were multiplied by a maid, Esmeralda (Alice Ghostley), a witch with diminishing powers, and by his and Sam's first child, Tabitha, who inherited her mother's magical gifts.

Bewitched was an instant hit, ranking as the second most watched series in its initial year. It was canceled in 1972 after eight seasons.

Bewitched (ABC), 1964–1972. Samantha Stevens/Serena: Elizabeth Montgomery, Darin Stevens: Dick York (1964–1969); Dick Sargeant (1969–1972), Endora: Agnes Moorehead, Larry Tate: David White, Aunt Clara: Marion Lorne (1964–1968), Uncle Arthur: Paul Lynde (1965–1972), Maurice: Maurice Evans, Dr. Bombay: Bernard Fox (1967–1972), Esmeralda: Alice Ghostley (1969–1972), Louise Tate: Irene Vernon (1964–1966); Kasey Rogers (1966–1972), Gladys Kravitz: Alice Pearce (1964–1966); Sandra Gould (1966–1972), Abner Kravitz: George Tobias, Tabitha Stevens: Heidi and Laura Gentry (1966); Tamar and Julie Young (1966); Erin and Diane Murphy (1966–1972), Adam Stevens: David and Greg Lawrence (1971–1972).

"Hey, hey, we're the Monkees," proclaim the "pre-fab four" just before their series' debut. They are (l. to r.) Davy Jones, Michael Nesmith, Mickey Dolenz, and Peter Tork.

The Monkees

Inspired by the antics of the Beatles in the movies *A Hard Day's Night* and *Help!*, producers Bert Schneider and Bob Rafelson decided to create a weekly TV series centered around a young rock band of mop-haired innocents similar to the irrepressible John, Paul, George, and Ringo.

The producers auditioned more than 400 applicants before choosing their pre-fab four: Davy Jones, a cute Englishman and former jockey; Mickey Dolenz, a former child actor who had starred in the TV show *Circus Boy*; Peter Tork, a one-time folk musician; and Michael Nesmith, a folk musician whose mother invented Liquid Paper.

Premiering on NBC in 1966, *The Monkees* utilized slow-motion, fast-motion, distorted focus, non sequiturs, and several other techniques rarely seen on TV shows. The group rambled with casual aplomb through the bizarre calamities that always seemed to beset them, invariably escaping the evil manipulators who lurked in their path.

Each episode featured a couple of songs. In the show, the Monkees appeared to be musicians, but on the recordings of their numbers, they only contributed the vocals. The instrumentals were handled by highly paid studio musicians employed by producer Don Kirshner. As for the songs, they were penned by top-notch songwriters, such as Neil Diamond ("I'm a Believer"). Consequently, the resulting albums sold in the millions.

By the second season, group members had begun to grumble about how they were manipulated and how they manipulated the public. The show was canceled in 1968 after its second year. In the late 1980s, three members of the original group, joined by Michael Nesmith on a few dates, reunited for a successful tour.

The Monkees (NBC), 1966–1968. Davy: Davy Jones, Peter: Peter Tork, Mickey: Mickey Dolenz, Mike: Michael Nesmith.

McHale's Navy

McHale's Navy (ABC), 1962–1966. Lt. Cmdr. Quinton McHale: Ernest Borgnine, Capt. Wallace B. Binghamton: Joe Flynn, Ensign Chuck Parker: Tim Conway, Lester Gruber: Carl Ballantine, George "Christy" Christopher: Gary Vinson, Harrison "Tinker" Bell: Billy Sands, Lt. Elroy Carpenter: Bob Hastings, Happy Haines: Gavin MacLeod (1962–1964), Virgil Edwards: Edson Stroll, Willy Moss: John Wright (1964–1966), Fuji: Yoshio Yoda.

Veteran actor Ernest Borgnine, known primarily for portrayals of mean-spirited heavies in film roles, revealed his comic touch by starring in *McHale's Navy*. As sly, easygoing Lt. Cmdr. Quinton McHale, he led a group of naval cutups stationed in the South Pacific during World War II.

The 30-minute ABC series, which started in 1962, was set on the remote island of Taratupa. There the lazy hustlers of PT 73 spent their days gambling, trying to outfox their superior with a neverending round of harebrained schemes, and otherwise enjoying themselves in their tropical home. McHale won his crew's loyalty by ignoring regulations and even occasionally taking part in his men's spirited escapades. His unmilitary attitude earned him the wrath of uptight Capt. Binghamton (Joe Flynn), who spent most of his time dreaming of a promotion. But McHale's knowledge of the region made him invaluable, so there was little the haughty captain could do about his demeanor. Binghamton tried to bring order to the squad by assigning it an ensign, Chuck Parker (Tim Conway), but Parker turned out to be a naive, likable dolt who was easily manipulated by the cagey sailors of PT 73. Among the large crew were Billy Sands as "Tinker" Bell and Gavin MacLeod as Happy Haines.

In the show's fourth and final season, McHale, Binghamton, Parker, and the rest of the gang were transferred to the small Italian town of Voltafiore, where they were to guard against a Nazi invasion. The town's mayor, Mario Lugatto (Jay Novello), was also a sharp con who quickly linked up with the sailors to add to the captain's headaches. The show was canceled in 1966.

Academy-award-winning actor Ernest Borgnine (right) departed from his usual bad guy roles to play the sensible, easy-going skipper of a crew of cutups in McHale's Navy. Behind him is Tim Conway, who played the bumbling Ensign Parker.

The Beverly Hillbillies

The Beverly Hillbillies ranks as the most successful situation comedy of the 1960s. The 30-minute CBS series, which premiered in 1962, followed an impoverished family from deep Appalachia to Beverly Hills, California, where they settled after the discovery of oil on their property had made them rich.

Family patriarch Jed Clampett (Buddy Ebsen) was a sensible, simple man, amused and occasionally confounded by the ways of modern American society, especially the conceits of the California elite. A widower, Clampett was joined in his move by three kinfolk, as he called them—his mother-in-law, Granny (Irene Ryan), a crusty old-timer who refused to give up her backwoods traditions; his daughter, Elly Mae Clampett (Donna Douglas), a gorgeous, naive blond who loved "critters," from dogs and cats to goats and skunks; and cousin Jethro Bodine (Max Baer, Jr.), a strapping young man who was as dumb as he was thick and who constantly concocted scatterbrained schemes to turn himself into a Hollywood bigshot.

Leading the family of Appalachian hillbillies trying to adjust to the good life in southern California was song-and-dance-man Buddy Ebsen as Jed Clampett. Jed's feisty mother-in-law, Granny, was played by veteran film actress Irene Ryan.

Elly Mae's (Donna Douglas, right) fondness for "critters" seems to have landed the hillbillies in trouble once again. Banker Milburn Drysdale (Raymond Bailey, left) tries to solve the problem with Elly Mae's cousin, Jethro Bodine (Max Baer, Jr.) and Drysdale's assistant, Jane Hathaway (Nancy Kulp).

Other regular cast members included Milburn Drysdale, president of Commerce Bank, where the Clampetts deposited their $25 million. To protect the unworldly family from swindlers, Drysdale convinced the Clampetts to move into the mansion next to his, much to the consternation of his snobbish wife, Margaret (Harriet MacGibbon). Drysdale also used his assistant, the prudish, efficient Jane Hathaway, to tend to the hillbillies' needs.

The series was an immediate smash, ranking as TV's top-rated program its first two seasons and attracting an average of 60 million viewers per week. In the Nielsen rankings of the most watched 30-minute programs in TV history, episodes of *The Beverly Hillbillies* account for the top eight. *The Beverly Hillbillies* fell from the Top 20 for the first time in 1971, the year the show was canceled.

The Beverly Hillbillies (CBS), 1962–1971. Jed Clampett: Buddy Ebsen, Granny: Irene Ryan, Elly May Clampett: Donna Douglas, Jethro Bodine: Max Baer, Jr., Milburn Drysdale: Raymond Bailey, Jane Hathaway: Nancy Kulp, Margaret Drysdale: Harriet MacGibbon, Cousin Pearl Bodine: Bea Benaderet (1962–1963), Sonny Drysdale: Louis Nye (1962), John Brewster: Frank Wilcox, Edythe Brewster: Lisa Seagram, Dash Riprock: Larry Pennell (1965–1969), Janet Trego: Sharon Tate (1963–1965).

The Petries' home life in a Manhattan suburb was exactly what many Americans wanted for themselves in the New Frontier years. Here Laura (Mary Tyler Moore) and Rob (Dick Van Dyke) attempt to deal with their son Richie's sudden use of bad language. The youngster was played by Larry Matthews.

The Dick Van Dyke Show

Dick Van Dyke was a one-time game show host who went on to star in the Broadway musical, *Bye Bye Birdie*. In 1961, he returned to television playing Rob Petrie in the 30-minute CBS series, *The Dick Van Dyke Show*.

Petrie was the head comedy writer for *The Alan Brady Show*, working with his wise-cracking good friends Sally Rogers (Rose Marie) and Buddy Sorrell (Morey Amsterdam). He also enjoyed a good marriage with a former dancer, Laura Petrie (Mary Tyler Moore in her first major role). They lived in New Rochelle, a suburb of New York, with their young son, Richie (Larry Matthews).

The plots, for the most part, involved either the shenanigans of Petrie and his co-workers or the copywriter's home life in the suburbs. At work, the co-workers regularly targeted their jokes at pompous producer, Melvin Cooley (Richard Deacon). They also lived in fear of the wrath of the often heard, rarely seen Alan Brady (Carl Reiner, the *Dick Van Dyke Show*'s creator and chief writer). At home, Petrie often got into mishaps at the behest of his friend and neighbor, Jerry Helper (Jerry Paris).

The series started slowly, but by its third season it ranked third in the year-end ratings. It remained in the Top 20 until 1966 when Van Dyke ended the show to pursue movie work full time. Four years later, Moore starred in her own successful series, where she also worked behind the scenes in television.

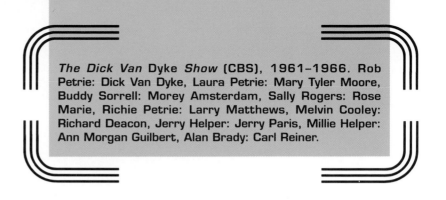

The Dick Van Dyke Show (CBS), 1961–1966. Rob Petrie: Dick Van Dyke, Laura Petrie: Mary Tyler Moore, Buddy Sorrell: Morey Amsterdam, Sally Rogers: Rose Marie, Richie Petrie: Larry Matthews, Melvin Cooley: Richard Deacon, Jerry Helper: Jerry Paris, Millie Helper: Ann Morgan Guilbert, Alan Brady: Carl Reiner.

Rob's frolicsome co-writers on *The Alan Brady Show* were Buddy Sorrell (Morey Amsterdam, center) and Sally Rogers (Rose-Marie). The show's producer, Mel Cooley (Richard Deacon), was the neverending butt of Buddy's jokes.

In high camp style, the Dynamic Duo, Robin (Burt Ward, left) and Batman (Adam West) battled crime in Gotham City. In an unusual programming move, their show aired twice a week, in 30-minute segments.

Batman

Bob Kane created the cartoon super-hero Batman in 1939 for Detective Comics. Through the 1940s, the character was featured on radio and in two movie serials. Then, in 1966, ABC brought *Batman* to television, running it in two-part stories on consecutive evenings.

The story line followed the theme of the comic book. Bruce Wayne (Adam West) was an orphan who avenged the violent deaths of his parents by using their fortune to design a sophisticated, underground crime lab in the basement of his mansion, Wayne Manor. He

At home, widower Andy Taylor enjoyed the company of Aunt Bee (Frances Bavier), who tended his house, and his young son, Opie (Ron Howard).

Get Smart

Get Smart (NBC), 1965–1969; (CBS), 1969–1970.
Maxwell Smart: Don Adams, Agent 99: Barbara Feldon,
The Chief: Edward Platt, Hymie the Robot: Dick Gautier
(1966–1969), Larraby: Robert Karvelas (1967–1970),
Conrad Siegfried: Bernie Koppell (1966–1969), Starker:
King Moody (1966–1969), Agent 13: Dave Ketchum
(1966–1967), Agent 44: Victor French, Carlson: Stacy
Keach (1966–1967), 99's Mother: Jane Dulo
(1968–1969).

Get Smart was a spoof of the secret agent genre, sparked by the James Bond movies and their several film and television successors. Premiering on NBC in 1965, *Get Smart* was also one of the few successful 30-minute comedies not centered around a family.

The series starred Don Adams as secret agent Maxwell Smart, a well-meaning but bumbling operative for the government agency CONTROL. Smart, also known as Agent 86, blundered his way through every caper yet somehow always managed to disrupt the diabolical plans for world domination hatched by the madmen of an underground group known as KAOS. Smart often received assistance from his alluring partner, the cool-headed Agent 99 (Barbara Feldon). He also regularly confounded his superior, known only as the Chief (Edward Platt).

Smart, like other super-agents, relied on sophisticated gadgets. In his case, though, they rarely worked as planned. One such device was a phone hidden in the sole of his shoe, which tended to ring at the wrong moments. His colleagues also proved nearly as inept as he was. They included dim-witted agent Larraby (Robert Karvelas), Hymie the Robot (Dick Gautier), Agent 13 (Dave Ketchum), and Agent 44 (Victor French).

Get Smart ran for four seasons on NBC before switching to CBS. During the final season on NBC, Smart and 99 finally fell in love and were married. The following year, 99 gave birth to twins. The series was canceled in 1970.

Despite his incredible bunglings, agent Maxwell Smart (Don Adams) always managed to foil KAOS's schemes for world domination. In this, he was assisted by the poised and beautiful Agent 99 (Barbara Feldon).

As this photo suggests, being a castaway wasn't all bad. The three Gilligan's Island regulars pictured here are (l. to r.) Alan Hale, Jr. as the Skipper, Tina Louise as Ginger Grant, and Bob Denver as Gilligan.

Gilligan's Island

Gilligan's Island followed the comic exploits of seven people marooned in the South Pacific after their small charter boat crashed on the shore of an unknown isle during a tropical storm. Bob Denver played Gilligan, the buffoonish crewman of the *Minnow* who spent most of the show's episodes concocting lame-brained schemes designed to get the hapless castaways off the island. The only other crew member was the boat's captain, Jonas Grumby (Alan Hale, Jr.). A congenial older man, the Skipper, as he was called, referred to his bumbling-but-lovable first mate as "my little buddy." However, he constantly grew infuriated at Gilligan's exploits.

The rest of the castaways were rather one-dimensional caricatures. There was the sexy Hollywood starlet, Ginger Grant (Tina Louise), who owned an endless supply of skimpy cocktail gowns and was concerned primarily with her own appearance; the high school science teacher known as the Professor (Russell Johnson), an absent-minded tinkerer always involved in some homemade experiment; Mary Ann Summers (Dawn Wells), a naive young woman from the rural South; Thurston Howell III (Jim Backus), a stingy, pompous billionaire; and the billionaire's wife, Lovey Howell (Natalie Schafer), a dim-witted name-dropper.

The 30-minute CBS series, which premiered in 1964, quickly attracted a large following, especially among children. After keeping the seven strangers stranded for three full seasons, *Gilligan's Island* was canceled in 1967. Most of the cast was reunited for several TV movies, starting with *Rescue from Gilligan's Island* in 1978.

Gilligan's Island (CBS), 1964–1967. Gilligan: Bob Denver, the Skipper (Jonas Grumby): Alan Hale, Jr., Ginger Grant: Tina Louise, the Professor (Roy Hinkley): Russell Johnson, Mary Ann Summers: Dawn Wells, Thurston Howell III: Jim Backus, Lovey Howell: Natalie Schafer.

disguised himself as Batman with a mask, a cape, and a colorful leotard, and then fought crime with an arsenal of high-tech devices. He was assisted by his young ward, the orphaned Dick Grayson (Burt Ward). Batman was known as the Caped Crusader, Grayson as Robin the Boy Wonder, and together they were the Dynamic Duo.

To protect Gotham City, the two were often summoned by Police Commissioner Gordon (Neil Hamilton) and Chief O'Hara (Stafford Repp) by a special Batphone or by a searchlight known as the Batsignal. The duo scooted to crimes at rocket speed in the specially equipped Batmobile.

What particularly distinguished this series was its high camp style and the numerous guest stars who appeared as the Dynamic Duo's bizarre archenemies. They included Burgess Meredith as the Penguin, Cesar Romero as the Joker, Frank Gorshin as the Riddler (later played by John Astin), Victor Buono as King Tut, Julie Newmar as Catwoman, (later played by Eartha

Kitt and Lee Ann Meriwether), Milton Berle as Louie the Lilac, and Tallulah Bankhead as the Black Widow.

The series premiered as a midseason replacement in January 1966. In its first year, the two weekly programs both ranked among the Top 10 shows. By the second year, however, the ratings had slipped. ABC cut the show to once a week and added a third crime fighter, Batgirl (Yvonne Craig), the secret identity of Barbara Gordon, Commissioner Gordon's daughter. The show was canceled in 1968 after two seasons.

A theatrical version of *Batman*, with a very different style than the series, was released in 1989.

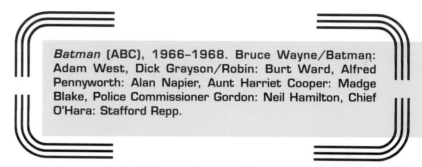

Batman (ABC), 1966–1968. Bruce Wayne/Batman: Adam West, Dick Grayson/Robin: Burt Ward, Alfred Pennyworth: Alan Napier, Aunt Harriet Cooper: Madge Blake, Police Commissioner Gordon: Neil Hamilton, Chief O'Hara: Stafford Repp.

During the 1967–1968 season, Batman and Robin were joined by a third crime fighter, Batgirl (Yvonne Craig), who was really Barbara Gordon, Commissioner Gordon's daughter.

Among the diabolical archfiends who confronted the Dynamic Duo, perhaps none was peskier than the Penguin, played with panache by Burgess Meredith. Playing <u>Batman</u> baddies became an "in thing" among Hollywood's veterans.

COVER CHARGE
$100.00

Only Rich People
and Friends
Admitted

The Andy Griffith Show

The hyperactive, overly zealous Barney Fife (Don Knotts, front) would have been enough to drive most anyone to violence but he never seemed to get the better of the even-tempered sheriff (Griffith), who is here simply showing his deputy a solid choke-hold.

The Andy Griffith Show premiered on CBS in 1960 and over eight seasons set the standard for gentle, homespun rural humor on television, thanks to a strong cast and wonderful scripts that highlighted the comic quirkiness of its citizens without depending on shallow southern stereotypes.

Griffith portrayed folksy sheriff Andy Taylor of the small, peaceful North Carolina town of Mayberry. Griffith's drawling, easygoing manner camouflaged a cagey intelligence and natural leadership qualities.

Since Mayberry encountered little crime, the 30-minute episodes focused on the relationships among its characters. Don Knotts won five Emmy awards for his portrayal of Barney Fife, a hyperactive deputy whose zealousness in enforcing the letter of the law continually landed him in embarrassing situations. Taylor, a widower, lived with his endearingly fussy Aunt Bee (Frances Bavier), who kept his house and helped him look after his young, red-headed son, Opie (Ron Howard).

The series launched Jim Nabors as Gomer Pyle, a naive, good-natured gas station attendant who joined the show in 1963 and left two years later to star in a spinoff, Gomer Pyle, U.S.M.C. He was replaced by George Lindsey as cousin Goober Pyle. Other townsfolk included the local lush, Otis Campbell (Hal Smith), barber Floyd Lawson (Howard McNear), handyman Emmet Clark (Paul Hartman), and town clerk Howard Sprague (Jack Dodson). Barney's girlfriend, Thelma Lou, was played by Betty Lynn, and Andy's gal, Helen Crump, whom he eventually married, was Aneta Corsaut.

The series, which began as an episode on The Danny Thomas Show, ranked among the Top 10 shows in each of its eight years, and was the number-one rated program on TV when Griffith left in 1968 (Knotts had departed in 1965). The series was then transformed into Mayberry, R.F.D. with Ken Berry playing a widower and town councilman.

The Andy Griffith Show (CBS), 1960–1968. Andy Taylor: Andy Griffith, Barney Fife: Don Knotts (1960–1965), Opie Taylor: Ron Howard, Aunt Bee Taylor: Frances Bavier, Gomer Pyle: Jim Nabors (1963–1964), Goober Pyle: George Lindsey (1965–1968), Helen Crump: Aneta Corsaut (1964–1968), Thelma Lou: Betty Lynn (1960–1965), Floyd Lawson: Howard McNear, Otis Campbell: Hal Smith (1960–1967), Howard Sprague: Jack Dodson (1966–1968), Emmett Clark: Paul Hartman (1966–1967), Clara Edwards: Hope Summers, Warren Ferguson: Jack Burns (1965–1966).

I Dream of Jeannie

Back home in Cocoa Beach, Florida, Jeannie (Eden) creates a host of problems for the bachelor astronaut (Hagman, left). Here the duo play host to a celebrated guest star, Sammy Davis, Jr.

Larry Hagman, in his first major television role, starred as Air Force astronaut Tony Nelson, who was on a space mission when an emergency forced him to parachute to safety on an isolated island. While waiting for a rescue team, he discovered an elaborately embellished bottle on the shore. He opened the lid and, lo and behold, out jumped a beautiful genie named Jeannie (Barbara Eden), who immediately pronounced Nelson her "master" since he had liberated her.

The astronaut carried Jeannie, hidden inside her small but lushly appointed bottle, back to Cocoa Beach, Florida, his base and home. There, he tried to convince his superiors that he had found an authentic genie with magical powers, but no one would believe him. The base psychiatrist, the self-important Dr. Alfred Bellows (Hayden Rorke), even concluded that Nelson suffered from hallucinations brought on by exposure to the sun. Jeannie aggravated Nelson's problems by disappearing whenever anyone else came near. Eventually, his best friend and fellow astronaut, Roger Healey (Bill Daily), learned of Jeannie's presence, but the knowledge only served to make him envious of his friend's command over a gorgeous, supple woman.

Most of the *I Dream of Jeannie* episodes revolved around the confusion Jeannie caused in Nelson's life and her inability to grasp middle American culture. The show, which premiered in 1965, lasted five seasons, long enough to see Nelson and Healey promoted from captains to majors and to see Jeannie and Nelson married during the show's final year. A made-for-TV reunion film aired in 1991 with Eden and Daily but without Hagman, who had gone on to bigger things in the intervening years.

I Dream of Jeannie (NBC), 1965–1970. Jeannie: Barbara Eden, Capt. Tony Nelson: Larry Hagman, Capt. Roger Healey: Bill Daily, Dr. Alfred Bellows: Hayden Rorke, Amanda Bellows: Emmaline Henry (1966–1970), Gen. Martin Peterson: Barton MacLane (1965–1969), Gen. Wingard Stone: Philip Ober (1965–1966), Melissa Stone: Karen Sharpe (1965–1966), Gen. Winfield Shaeffer: Vinton Hayworth (1969–1970).

Stranded on an isolated island after his space mission is aborted, astronaut Tony Nelson (Larry Hagman) enjoys the ministrations of a centuries-old genie (Barbara Eden) whom he has freed from a bottle.

Bedrock's favorite couple—Fred and Wilma Flintstone—enjoy an outing in the family car. Hanna-Barbera's clever prehistoric interpretations of 20th-century technological advances were among the highlights of the series.

The Flintstones

The Flintstones premiered in 1960 as the first animated prime-time comedy in television history. So far, it has turned out to be the longest-running evening cartoon series as well. Produced by TV cartoon kings William Hanna and Joseph Barbera, the show, which seemed inspired by *The Honeymooners*, parodied modern suburban life while taking place in the Stone Age.

Fred and Wilma Flintstone resided in Bedrock, along with their best friends and next-door neighbors, Barney and Betty Rubble. The plots blended prehistoric puns with the concerns of common Americans: the vacuum cleaner was a baby elephant, the garbage disposal was a starving buzzard, the lawn mower was a grass-eating dinosaur on wheels, and the record player was a bird whose long beak served as the needle. Fred worked at the Rock Head & Quarry Cave Construction Co., lived in a well-kept cave, and drove a car powered by his own legs. The Flintstones started with a pet dinosaur named Dino, then in 1962 gained a pony-tailed baby daughter, Pebbles. The Rubbles, not to be outdone, adopted a club-wielding boy named Bamm Bamm.

The show also enjoyed creating takeoffs of other pop culture icons. Among those making appearances over the years were Ann Margrock, Gina Lollobrickada, lawyer Perry Masonry (who always won his cases), "really big" TV host Ed Sullystone, and the Gruesome Family, a strange couple modeled on the Addams Family.

The Flintstones, along with the animated *Beany and Cecil*, became ABC's first all-color series in 1962. The series landed among the Top 20 in its first season and remained on the air for six years. It was canceled in 1966.

In 1962, Fred and Wilma's neighbors, Barney and Betty Rubble, adopted a club-wielding child called Bamm Bamm, who is seen here giving his father a lift.

The Flintstones (ABC), 1960–1966. (voices) Fred Flintstone: Alan Reed, Wilma Flintstone: Jean vander Pyl, Barney Rubble: Mel Blanc, Betty Rubble: Bea Benaderet (1960–1964); Gerry Johnson (1964–1966), Pebbles: Jean vander Pyl, Bamm Bamm: Don Messick, Dino: Mel Blanc.

Charles Addams originally created a cast of ghoulish, bizarre family members for a series of cartoons in *The New Yorker* magazine. In 1964, when the characters were transformed into a 30-minute situation comedy for ABC-TV, the cartoonist gave them names, and the Addams Family was born.

Carolyn Jones starred as the matron of the haunted house, Morticia Frump Addams, a seductive, elegantly warped wife and mother. John Astin portrayed her husband, lawyer Gomez Addams, who was passionate about everything—from smoking cigars to kissing the length of Morticia's arm to setting up violent crashes on his model train sets.

Other household members included Jackie Coogan as Uncle Fester, the hairless crackpot who could light a bulb by putting it in his mouth; six-foot-nine-inch Ted Cassidy as Lurch, the Frankenstein-like butler whose vocabulary consisted primarily of "You rang?" and a deep-toned grunt; Blossom Rock as Gomez's mother, Grandmama, a witch; Lisa Loring as Wednesday Addams, the cruel, unemotional young daughter; Ken Weatherwax as Pugsley Addams, the chubby, destructive son; Felix Silla as Cousin Itt, a midget covered from head to toe by hair; and Thing, a disembodied hand that popped out of a black box.

The series lasted two years. By coincidence, *The Munsters*, a situation comedy on CBS about another amusingly gruesome family, also premiered in 1964 and ended in 1966. A theatrical movie based on Addams' cartoons and the series was released in 1991, with Raul Julia as Gomez and Anjelica Huston as Morticia.

The Addams Family (ABC), 1964–1966. Morticia Addams: Carolyn Jones, Gomez Addams: John Astin, Uncle Fester: Jackie Coogan, Wednesday Thursday Addams: Lisa Loring, Pugsley Addams: Ken Weatherwax, Lurch: Ted Cassidy, Grandmama Addams: Blossom Rock, Cousin Itt: Felix Silla, Thing: Ted Cassidy.

The Addams Family

My Favorite Martian

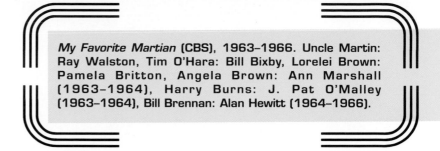

My Favorite Martian (CBS), 1963–1966. Uncle Martin: Ray Walston, Tim O'Hara: Bill Bixby, Lorelei Brown: Pamela Britton, Angela Brown: Ann Marshall (1963–1964), Harry Burns: J. Pat O'Malley (1963–1964), Bill Brennan: Alan Hewitt (1964–1966).

M y *Favorite Martian* paired a calm, even-keeled young journalist with a mischievous Martian he happened to stumble upon while on assignment. Bill Bixby starred as Tim O'Hara, a news reporter for the Los Angeles *Sun*, who witnessed a spaceship as it crashed to Earth. Thinking he had the scoop of a lifetime, he rescued the disoriented alien, played by veteran character actor Ray Walston. However, there was a catch: the Martian looked human, spoke English, and let it be known that he would deny any story O'Hara wrote.

Thus, instead of making him the subject of a story, O'Hara befriended the charming alien, calling him Uncle Martin and allowing him to move into his home while he tried to repair his vessel. "Uncle Martin" may have looked human but he definitely wasn't. He could call upon little retractable antennae in the top of his head to become telepathic, he could levitate objects by pointing his finger at them, and he could become invisible. The plots dealt with the sticky situations that O'Hara found himself in because of his new roommate and purported relative.

Among the other regular cast members was Lorelei Brown (Pamela Britton), the owner of O'Hara's boardinghouse. Uncle Martin took a romantic interest in the widow, which created more problems, especially since she dated a suspicious policeman, detective Bill Brennan (Alan Hewitt).

The 30-minute CBS series premiered in 1963 and jumped into the year-end Top 10. However, the novelty fizzled quickly, and the show was canceled in 1966.

He had retractable antennae, could levitate objects, and could make himself invisible, but otherwise the Martian played by Ray Walston (left) in My Favorite Martian was the same as anyone else. His "nephew" in the series, Tim O'Hara, was Bill Bixby.

93

Hogan's Heroes

Hogan's Heroes proved that a popular situation comedy could be derived from almost any setting: the 30-minute CBS series was based on the exploits of a group of Allied soldiers imprisoned in a Nazi POW camp during World War II.

Bob Crane starred as the sly, quick-witted Col. Robert Hogan, who provided leadership to the motley crew of Stalag 13. Crane and his men continually outsmarted the camp's inept leader, the monocled Colonel Klink (Werner Klemperer), and his assistant, Sergeant Schultz (John Banner). Schultz was less pompous than his superior but just as dense and easily conned.

Crane and his men doctored the barbed-wire fence surrounding the camp so that they could come and go as they pleased. Moreover, their prison quarters were equipped like a resort, complete with a steam room and a topnotch chef. To rationalize their remaining in captivity, the plots regularly showed them feeding top-secret Nazi intelligence to the Allied forces. Thus they were more valuable as POWs than they would have been on the front lines.

Constantly outwitted by Hogan's band were the thick and thick-headed Sergeant Schultz (John Banner) and the pompous, but none too bright commandant, Colonel Klink (Werner Klemperer).

The prisoners included an equal opportunity cast of cutups, among them a British corporal, Peter Newkirk (Richard Dawson), a French corporal, Louis LeBeau (Robert Clary), an African-American sergeant, James Kinchloe (Ivan Dixon), and a rural American innocent, Sgt. Andrew Carter (Larry Hovis). As an interesting sidenote, Robert Clary had actually been imprisoned in a Nazi camp as a child. The series lasted six seasons before it was canceled in 1971.

Col. Robert Hogan (Bob Crane, center) played ringleader to an international group of POWs at Stalag 13 during World War II. Left of Crane is an African-American sergeant played by Ivan Dixon and opposite him is a French corporal played by Robert Clary. Clary had actually been imprisoned in a Nazi camp as a child.

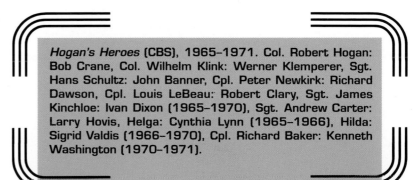

Hogan's Heroes (CBS), 1965–1971. Col. Robert Hogan: Bob Crane, Col. Wilhelm Klink: Werner Klemperer, Sgt. Hans Schultz: John Banner, Cpl. Peter Newkirk: Richard Dawson, Cpl. Louis LeBeau: Robert Clary, Sgt. James Kinchloe: Ivan Dixon (1965–1970), Sgt. Andrew Carter: Larry Hovis, Helga: Cynthia Lynn (1965–1966), Hilda: Sigrid Valdis (1966–1970), Cpl. Richard Baker: Kenneth Washington (1970–1971).

The breakthrough sitcom, *That Girl*, focused on the adventures of a young, career-oriented single woman in New York City. Here, Ann Marie (Marlo Thomas, left) watches aghast as her father (Lew Parker) and a neighbor (Betty Kean) try to pick the lock on her apartment door.

Marlo Thomas, who grew up watching her father, Danny, on television, climbed to stardom as the lead character of *That Girl*, among the first comedy series to feature an independent career woman as the lead character. The 30-minute ABC series premiered in 1966 with Thomas as Ann Marie, an ambitious, animated young woman who had left her middle-class home in Brewster, New York to pursue her dream of being an actress in New York City.

Always on the verge of a big break and constantly changing agents, Ann spent most of her time acting in TV commercials and playing bit parts in Off-Broadway plays. To make ends meet, she took a variety of clerical and sales jobs. During her first commercial, she met Don Hollinger (Ted Bessell), an equally young and ambitious writer for *Newsview* magazine. The two started a romance that would continue through all of the show's five seasons. They finally became engaged in 1970, but the series ended before the wedding could take place (but not before Don held his bachelor party, which led to a spat between him and Ann).

Regular cast members were few, although several actors had recurring roles. Ann's parents, Lou and Helen Marie (Lew Parker and Rosemary DeCamp), ran a restaurant. Her neighbors, Leon and Judy Bessemer (Dabney Coleman and Bonnie Scott), regularly checked on her. Bernie Kopell played Don's friend, Jerry Bauman, and Ann's agents included George Carlin, Ronnie Schell, and Morty Gunty. Danny Thomas also made several cameos on the series over the years.

That Girl

That Girl (ABC), 1966–1971. Ann Marie: Marlo Thomas, Don Hollinger: Ted Bessell, Lou Marie: Lew Parker, Helen Marie: Rosemary DeCamp (1966–1970), Leon Bessemer: Dabney Coleman (1966–1967), Judy Bessemer: Bonnie Scott (1966–1967), Jerry Bauman: Bernie Kopell, Ruth Bauman: Carolyn Daniels (1967–1969); Alice Borden (1969–1971), George Lester: George Carlin (1966–1967), Harvey Peck: Ronnie Schell (1966–1967).

The series followed the relationship between writer Don Hollinger (Ted Bessell) and Ann (Thomas) from their first meeting to their engagement. A 1970 episode found Ted training for the ring so that he could write an article on boxing.

Mister Ed featured the cranky comments of a talking horse (of course), demonstrating that creatures with more than two legs could participate in the silly fun of situation comedies. The 30-minute series started off as a syndicated production in 1961, but CBS quickly snatched the program for its prime-time lineup the same year.

As the series opened, a friendly, well-adjusted architect named Wilbur Post (Alan Young) had decided to move from the city to the countryside with his wife, Carol (Connie Hines). The couple bought an expansive ranch home, and when Post walked into the barn, he discovered that he had also purchased a handsome palomino—who could talk. The horse, Mister Ed, had apparently always had the gift of gab. But he had never talked to anyone before because he had never met anyone worth the effort. Then he encountered his new friend, Wilbur. Mister Ed continued to speak only to Post, which created scores of embarrassing situations for his owner. So did Mister Ed's other peculiarities, such as his hypochondria and acrophobia, as well as his wish for a horse-size bed and his desire to have his stall decorated in a Hawaiian motif.

The only other regular cast members were the Post's neighbors. For the first two seasons, they were Roger and Kay Addison (Larry Keating and Edna Skinner). Actor Keating succumbed to a heart attack in 1963, and for the show's final two seasons the Posts acquired new neighbors, Gordon and Winnie Kirkwood (Leon Ames and Florence MacMichael). The series ended its prime-time run in 1965, then lasted one season on Sunday afternoons.

Mister Ed

Mister Ed (CBS), 1961–1965. Wilbur Post: Alan Young, Carol Post: Connie Hines, Voice of Mister Ed: Allan "Rocky" Lane, Roger Addison: Larry Keating (1961–1963), Kay Addison: Edna Skinner (1961–1964), Gordon Kirkwood: Leon Ames (1963–1965), Winnie Kirkwood: Florence MacMichael (1963–1965).

Variety Shows

Much of the appeal of The Dean Martin Show stemmed from the host's casual, relaxed manner, which comes across even in this still photo of him with singer Lena Horne.

The Dean Martin Show

Veteran singer-actor Dean Martin brought a casual, low-key flair to the variety format, acting as if he had invited the camera and audience to his house for an evening cocktail party featuring music, jokes, and informal chats. Even the set was designed to look like a living room.

The tone of *The Dean Martin Show*, which started on NBC in 1965, emerged because of the star's contract, which stipulated that he devote only one day a week to rehearsals and taping. But it proved successful. Each program was loose and laid back, much like Martin's personality, and the audience loved it.

In the beginning, Martin's only regular cast member was pianist Ken Lane. Then, in 1967, a group of young female dancers, the Golddiggers, came aboard. Three years later, an evolving collection of singers and comics—among them Kay Medford, Marian Mercer, Lou Jacobi, Tom Bosley, Nipsey Russell, Dom DeLuise, Rodney Dangerfield, and Foster Brooks—began appearing regularly. Most of them stayed with the show for a year and then left.

In 1973, the show and format changed. It became *The Dean Martin Comedy Hour*, and the cast was pared back to Martin and Lane. Each program featured two weekly segments: one was a celebrity roast, with a lineup of wits sitting at a head banquet table, taking turns tossing barbs at the guest of honor and at each other; the other segment spotlighted a country music star.

The new format lasted only one year. Then the show was canceled after nine seasons.

(Preceding page) Harvey Korman and Carol Burnett of The Carol Burnett Show.

The Dean Martin Show (NBC), 1965–1974. Host: Dean Martin, Regulars: Ken Lane, The Golddiggers (1967–1971), Kay Medford (1970–1973), Marian Mercer (1971–1972), Lou Jacobi (1971–1973), Tom Bosley (1971–1972), Nipsey Russell (1972–1973), Dom DeLuise (1972–1973), Rodney Dangerfield (1972–1973).

The Golddiggers joined the show in 1967. Here, they are joined by Dean (right), Hermione Baddeley (upper right), and Abe Vigoda to pay tribute to the Roaring 20s.

Part of what made _The Judy Garland Show_ so special were the guest stars, many of whom appeared infrequently on television. One program featured the multitalented Donald O'Connor, who, like Judy, was a veteran of the MGM stable.

The Judy Garland Show

Judy Garland starred in a highly successful special in the spring of 1963, which gave CBS the idea of putting her in a weekly series that could perhaps pull some of the audience away from the extremely popular *Bonanza* on Sunday nights. Thus, *The Judy Garland Show* premiered in September 1963 opposite TV's highest-rated series.

At first, Garland's variety hour used the special as a model, primarily showcasing the star's musical talents in expensive production numbers. When that concept failed, a new producer was hired and a folksier format was introduced. It featured Garland interacting and conversing with guests. By the end of the year, four producers and an equal number of formats had been tested on the audience, but all of them had failed to dent the *Bonanza* stranglehold on the hour.

For the first few months, Jerry Van Dyke was a regular cast member, and musical advisor Mel Tormé made frequent guest appearances. Ken Murray was added after Van Dyke left, and he hosted a segment that took cameras into the homes of celebrities for brief interviews and tours. The highlights, however, were Garland's performances and her dazzling guests. They included Ray Bolger, Garland's co-star in *The Wizard of Oz*; Mickey Rooney, her former child-star cohort in several MGM movies; Broadway legend Ethel Merman; the new singing sensation, Barbra Streisand; and daughters Liza Minnelli and Lorna Luft.

The show's final two months primarily featured Garland, without guests or other cast members. Those programs are now considered classics. The series was canceled in March 1964.

After a number of formats for The Judy Garland Show had failed to draw viewers away from Bonanza as CBS had hoped, the final programs simply featured the show's star all by herself, doing what she did best.

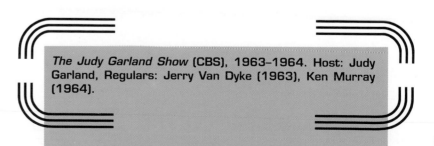

The Judy Garland Show (CBS), 1963–1964. Host: Judy Garland, Regulars: Jerry Van Dyke (1963), Ken Murray (1964).

The Tonight Show Starring Johnny Carson

Johnny Carson had been a magician ("The Great Carsoni"), a radio and television announcer, a comedy writer, a quiz show host, and a serious actor when he was invited to substitute for host Jack Paar on *The Tonight Show* in 1958. Four years later, when Paar left the program in a dispute, NBC called the genial Midwesterner and asked him to try a stint as the regular host.

Unlike Paar, who was mercurial and combative, Carson was congenial and clever. He bantered with celebrities in an easygoing, non-patronizing style, and offered up quick quips that never involved pot shots at his guests. He gradually developed a relaxed, assured monologue to open the nightly program, and he created an array of comical characters that he sometimes used for laughs before introducing his guests. He met sidekick Ed McMahon in 1958 when the two worked on the same quiz show, *Who Do You Trust?* The two have worked together on *The Tonight Show* since Carson's debut in October 1962.

Game show host Johnny Carson brought congeniality and quick wit to The Tonight Show. As a result, the program changed dramatically from the "sturm und drang" of the Paar years.

When Carson began, the nightly series originated in New York and was taped for West Coast broadcast. In 1972, the program moved to Burbank. At first, it was taped the day before it aired, but the delay cost the show its sense of immediacy, so the tapings started taking place late in the afternoon for nationwide telecast that same night.

Relations between Carson and the network haven't always been perfect. The host walked off the show in a contract dispute in 1967 but was lured back with a $1-million-a-year deal. In 1978, his salary rose to $3 million. Two years later, as a further concession, the 90-minute show was trimmed to an hour. Still, the time for leaving finally came. In 1991, Carson announced his plan to retire as *The Tonight Show* host, saying he'd leave the following year, after his 30th anniversary with the program. Comedian Jay Leno, who had become Carson's permanent substitute host after Joan Rivers left the show for her own late-night talk show, was tapped as his replacement.

This photo of more recent vintage shows a Carson who is clearly older, but the setup is fundamentally the same as it was when he joined The Tonight Show in 1962—the host is seated behind his desk, coffee cup nearby, and his long-time sidekick, Ed McMahon, is leading the laughs.

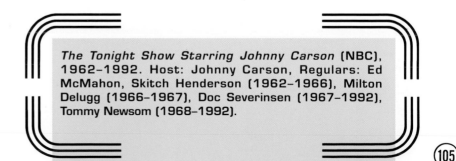

The Tonight Show Starring Johnny Carson (NBC), 1962–1992. Host: Johnny Carson, Regulars: Ed McMahon, Skitch Henderson (1962–1966), Milton Delugg (1966–1967), Doc Severinsen (1967–1992), Tommy Newsom (1968–1992).

Durward Kirby (left) and Allan Funt gleefully watch the results of the Candid Camera gang's latest gag. Funt originated the idea of airing people's spontaneous reactions to bizarre situations when he was in the armed forces during World War II.

Candid Camera

It was while he was in the armed forces during World War II that Allen Funt created the idea of recording the candid reactions of unsuspecting people. He began by secretly taping his fellow soldiers as they griped about life in the service and then airing their comments on Armed Forces Radio. Later, as a civilian, he sold a radio program called *Candid Microphone* to ABC. He had gone big-time, but the concept was the same—taping people's responses to strange questions and then broadcasting the results.

In 1948, ABC convinced Funt to hide a camera along with his microphone and thus a network version of his series was born. The TV show remained *Candid Microphone* until Funt moved to NBC in 1949. At that time, the name became *Candid Camera*.

The premise of the TV program was simple: Funt and his crew would contrive a bizarre situation and then catch an unsuspecting person as he or she stepped into the trap. The victim's reaction was often hilarious. Imagine, for example, arriving at the Pennsylvania–Delaware border and being told by the guard that Delaware was closed for the day; or rolling your bowling ball down a lane and having it come back without the holes; or being a gas station attendant confronted by a customer who is having trouble starting his car, then lifting up the hood and finding no engine. These were just a few of the classic setups that Funt and his writers created over the years.

Candid Camera ran for brief periods on all three networks from 1948 to 1950, becoming a segment of *The Garry Moore Show* in 1959. A year later, Funt was given his own 30-minute prime-time spot on CBS, and this outing earned *Candid Camera* its great popularity and renown.

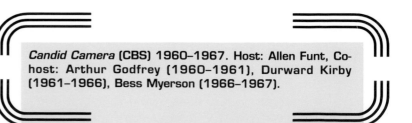

Candid Camera (CBS) 1960–1967. Host: Allen Funt, Co-host: Arthur Godfrey (1960–1961), Durward Kirby (1961–1966), Bess Myerson (1966–1967).

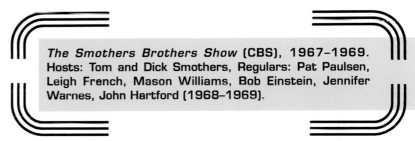

The Smothers Brothers Comedy Hour

CBS, in its continuing struggle to find a show to battle *Bonanza* on Sunday nights, decided in 1967 to develop a series appealing to the under-30 generation and to place it up against the aging Western. The network turned to the Smothers Brothers, a duo mixing comedy and folk music who had starred in a failed situation comedy two years earlier.

Tom Smothers played the guitar and acted like a stammering dullard who couldn't resist making vapid remarks to the neverending annoyance of his brother. Dick Smothers played the bass and portrayed the intelligent, reasonable sibling who struggled to maintain his self-control in the face of Tom's absurdities. For the most part, the program relied on irreverence and satire to poke fun at such American institutions as church, family, and government.

The Smothers Brothers Comedy Hour succeeded, at least in part, in helping CBS dethrone *Bonanza*. It broke into the Top 20 over the first year, causing NBC's Western to slip a few notches from the front runner's spot.

But the *Comedy Hour* created another problem for CBS, as the network constantly battled with the Smothers Brothers over their politically pointed humor and antiwar bent. During the run of the show, several skits were censored, to the brothers' dismay. Ironically, one of the routines dealt with film censorhip. The network also stopped the show from airing an interview with Dr. Benjamin Spock, who assisted draft resisters, and banned Pat Paulsen's tongue-in-cheek campaign for president until after the election.

CBS's purges also included cutting Pete Seeger singing a Vietnam protest song; Harry Belafonte singing before a film montage of the riots at the 1968 Democratic convention; and Joan Baez dedicating a song to her husband, who was imprisoned as a draft dodger.

Finally, near the end of the second season, the network abruptly canceled the series, although its ratings were still high.

The Smothers Brothers Show (CBS), 1967–1969. Hosts: Tom and Dick Smothers, Regulars: Pat Paulsen, Leigh French, Mason Williams, Bob Einstein, Jennifer Warnes, John Hartford (1968–1969).

After an unsuccessful sitcom, Dick Smothers (left) and his older brother Tom scored big with The Smothers Brothers Comedy Hour, but their brand of satire and topical humor brought them into frequent conflict with CBS, which yanked the show near the end of its second season.

By tradition, each season of <u>The Carol Burnett Show</u> opened with Jim Nabors as the special guest. Here the comic-singer (left) joins the show's star and regular Harvey Korman for a soft shoe.

The Carol Burnett Show

Carol Burnett worked her way up the television ladder before hosting the last successful, long-running variety show on the air. Her first TV role came in 1955, when she played the girlfriend of a ventriloquist's dummy on a Saturday morning show. Within a year, she had graduated to a prime-time leading role, that of Buddy Hackett's girlfriend in the short-lived situation comedy, *Stanley*.

From there, she cultivated a reputation as a singer of comic tunes, earning well-received guest spots on variety shows hosted by Garry Moore, Jack Parr, and Ed Sullivan. In 1959, she became a regular on the prime-time version of *The Garry Moore Show*, and the weekly spot allowed her to display her physically expressive comic ability and to develop a stock of hilarious, sometimes poignant characters.

In 1967, five years after she left the Moore show, CBS invited her to host her own variety program. For support, she gathered together a talented cast that included the versatile Harvey Korman, handsome straight man Lyle Waggoner, and newcomer Vicki Lawrence, who looked like Burnett's younger sister and sometimes played that role in skits. After Waggoner left in 1974, veteran comic actor Tim Conway joined the cast.

Burnett usually opened the show informally by announcing her guests and inviting questions from the studio audience. She ended on a similarly warm note, thanking her guests and pulling on her ear lobe—a signal to a relative—as she said goodnight. In between, she and her cast spoofed movies, other TV series, soap operas, and American families.

By 1975, only *The Ed Sullivan Show* and *Walt Disney* had run longer on prime-time television. That year, Korman left, and the ratings started to slip. Dick Van Dyke appeared as a regular for a few months in 1977, but departed when the ratings failed to pick up. The program was canceled in 1979 after 12 seasons.

The Carol Burnett Show (CBS), 1967–1979. Host: Carol Burnett, Regulars: Harvey Korman (1967–1977), Vicki Lawrence, Lyle Waggoner (1967–1974), Tim Conway (1975–1979), Dick Van Dyke (1977).

Among the most beloved of the funny yet poignant characters that Carol created was the washerwoman.

The Carol Burnett Show's movie parodies were among the highlights of the series, and none was better than this one, "Went with the Wind," featuring (l. to r.) Burnett, series regular Vicki Lawrence, and guest star Dinah Shore.

Rowan and Martin's Laugh-In

*R*owan & Martin's *Laugh-In* compiled a series of familiar comedy ideas into a frantic, innovative hour of short skits and one-liners. It not only proved to be an immediate hit with audiences, it also launched several careers.

In keeping with the quickly paced, gag-filled format of Laugh-In, *regulars and guest stars appeared in windows in the set to offer one-liners and humorous observations. Seen here are (l. to. r) hosts Dan Rowan and Dick Martin and series regular Goldie Hawn.*

Among the most memorable of Laugh-In's running gags was this one, which featured Ruth Buzzi as a crotchety old lady with a lethal purse and Arte Johnson as an ancient lecher.

Rowan & Martin's Laugh-In was rated the number one program in its first two seasons. In 1970, Carne, Hawn, Jo Anne Worley, and Dave Madden left the show. Johnson and Henry Gibson followed the next year. By then, the ratings had begun to slip. Finally, the show was canceled in 1973 after five seasons.

Rowan & Martin's Laugh-In (NBC), 1968–1973. Hosts: Dan Rowan and Dick Martin. Regulars: Ruth Buzzi, Judy Carne (1968–1970), Henry Gibson (1968–1971), Goldie Hawn (1968–1970), Arte Johnson (1968–1971), Dave Madden (1968–1969), Gary Owens, Alan Sues (1968–1972), Jo Anne Worley (1968–1970), Lily Tomlin (1970–1973).

Dan Rowan and Dick Martin were a veteran nightclub comedy duo who had never risen above B-team status until 1967, when they were given the role of hosting a one-time special for NBC called *Laugh-In*. Its success led the network to bring the show back as a midseason replacement series in January 1968, and then as a prime-time show that fall.

Each program spliced together a host of routines, repeating certain themes over and over. After a while, certain cast members became associated with specific gags, bits, and phrases: Judy Carne popularized the saying "Sock it to me," getting doused with water each time she said it; Lily Tomlin perfected a sarcastic, overbearing telephone operator named Ernestine and a precocious little girl known as Edith Ann; Ruth Buzzi played a spinster on a park bench who bopped a decrepit old man with her umbrella when he tried to snuggle up beside her; radio veteran Gary Owens mocked his profession by making his announcements in a hypermodulated voice while cupping a hand over his ear; Goldie Hawn portrayed a dizzy blonde with an infectious giggle; Arte Johnson was a Nazi soldier who peeked from behind potted palms and smirked, "Veery interesting—but stupid!" The audience came to know the characters and expected to see them in each episode. From time to time, celebrities were also taped doing bits. Richard Nixon, for example, was recorded saying "Sock it to me."

Periodically peeking up from the bushes at odd moments was this myopic, cigarette-smoking German soldier, played by Arte Johnson. He seemed to find everything "Veery interesting."

Acknowledgements

The producers of this book gratefully acknowledge the efforts of the National Broadcasting Company, the Columbia Broadcasting System, the American Broadcasting Company, the Public Broadcasting System, and the independent production companies, artists, writers, directors, technicians, musicians, and designers whose contribution to the television arts and sciences are celebrated in this book. Thanks, too, are due to Howard Mandelbaum and Ron Mandelbaum of Photofest, and to Harold Clarke of BDD Promotional Book Company, whose idea this was.

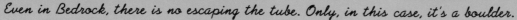

Even in Bedrock, there is no escaping the tube. Only, in this case, it's a boulder.